THE WRITINGS OF ATHENAGORAS

THE WRITINGS OF ATHENAGORAS

THE WRITINGS OF ATHENAGORAS
© Lighthouse Publishing 2018

All rights reserved. Without limiting the rights under copyright reserved above, no part of this publication may be reproduced, stored in a retrieval system, or transmitted, in any form or by any means (electronic, mechanical, photocopying, recording or otherwise), without the prior written permission of the copyright owner of this book.

Published by
Lighthouse Christian Publishing
SAN 257-4330
5531 Dufferin Drive
Savage, Minnesota, 55378
United States of America

www.lighthousechristianpublishing.com

Introductory Note to
THE WRITINGS OF ATHENAGORAS

[A.D. 177.] In placing Athenagoras here, somewhat out of the order usually accepted, I commit no appreciable violence against chronology, and I gain a great advantage for the reader. To some extent we must recognize, in collocation, the principles of affinity and historic growth. Closing up the bright succession of the earlier Apologists, this favorite author affords also a fitting introduction to the great founder of the Alexandrian School, who comes next into view. His work opens the way for Clement's elaboration of Justin's claim, that the whole of philosophy is embraced in Christianity. It is charming to find the primal fountains of Christian thought uniting here, to flow on for ever in the widening and deepening channel of Catholic orthodoxy, as it gathers into itself all human culture, and enriches the world with products of regenerated mind, harvested from its overflow into the fields of philosophy and poetry and art and science. More of this when we come to Clement, that man of genius who introduced Christianity to itself, as reflected in the burnished mirror of his intellect. Shackles are falling from the persecuted and imprisoned faculties of the faithful, and soon the Faith is to speak out, no more in tones of apology, but as mistress of the human mind, and its pilot to new worlds of discovery and broad domains of conquest. All hail the freedom with which, henceforth, Christians are to assume the overthrow of heathenism as a foregone conclusion. The distasteful exposure of heresies was the inevitable task after the first victory.

It was the chase and following-up of the adversary in his limping and cowardly retreat, "the scattering of the rear of darkness." With Athenagoras, we touch upon tokens of things to come; we see philosophy yoked to the chariot of Messiah; we begin to realize that sibylline surrender of outworn Paganism, and its forecast of an era of light: —

> "Magnus ab integro sæclorum nascitur ordo,
> .... quo ferrea primum
> Desinet, ac toto surget gens aurea mundo."

In Athenagoras, whose very name is a retrospect, we discover a remote result of St. Paul's speech on Mars Hill. The apostle had cast his bread upon the waters of Ilissus and Cephisus to find it after many days. "When they heard of the resurrection of the dead, some mocked;" but here comes a philosopher, from the Athenian *agora*, a convert to St. Paul's argument in his Epistle to the Corinthians, confessing "the unknown God," demolishing the marble mob of deities that so "stirred the apostle's spirit within him," and teaching alike the Platonist and the Stoic to sit at the feet of Jesus. "Dionysius the Areopagite, and the woman named Damaris," are no longer to be despised as the scanty first-fruits of Attica. They too have found a voice in this splendid trophy of the Gospel; and, "being dead, they yet speak" through him.

To the meager facts of his biography, which appear below, there is nothing to be added; and I shall restrain my disposition to be a commentator, within the limits of scanty notations. In the notes to Tatian and Theophilus, I have made the student acquainted with that useful addition to his treatise on *Justin Martyr*, in which the able and judicious Bishop Kaye harmonizes those authors with Justin. The same harmony enfolds the works of Athenagoras, and thus affords a synopsis of Christian teaching under the Antonines; in which precision of theological language is yet unattained, but identity of faith is clearly exhibited. While the Germans are furnishing the scholar with critical editions of the ancients, invaluable for their patient accumulations of fact and illustration, they are so daring in theory and conjecture when they come to exposition, that one enjoys the earnest and wholesome tone of sober comment that distinguishes the English theologian. It has the great merit of being inspired by profound sympathy with primitive writers, and unadulterated faith in the Scriptures. Too often a German critic treats one of these venerable witnesses, who yet live and yet speak, as if they were dead subjects on the dissecting-table. They cut and carve with anatomical display, and use the microscope with scientific skill; but, oh! how frequently they surrender the saints of God as mere corpses, into the hands of those who count them victims of a blind faith in a dead Christ.

It will not be necessary, after my quotations from Kaye in the foregoing sheets, to do more than indicate similar illustrations of Athenagoras to be found in his pages. The dry version often requires lubrications of devoutly fragrant exegesis; and providentially they are at hand in that elaborate but modest work, of which even this generation should not be allowed to lose sight.

The annotations of Conrad Gesner and Henry Stephans would have greatly enriched this edition, had I been permitted to enlarge the work by adding a version of them. They are often curious and are supplemented by the interesting letter of Stephans to Peter Nannius, "the eminent pillar of Louvain," on the earliest copies of Athenagoras, from which modern editions have proceeded. The Paris edition of Justin Marty (1615) contains these notes, as well as the Greek of Tatian, Theophilus, and Athenagoras, with a Latin rendering.
As Bishop Kaye constantly refers to this edition, I have considered myself fortunate in possessing it; using it largely in comparing his learned comments with the Edinburgh Version.

A few words as to the noble treatise of our author, on the Resurrection. As a firm and loving voice to this keynote of

Christian faith, it rings like an anthem through all the variations of his thought and argument. Comparing his own blessed hope with the delusions of a world lying in wickedness and looking steadfastly to the life of the world to come, what a sublime contrast we find in this figure of Christ's witness to the sensual life of the heathen, and even to the groping wisdom of the Attic sages. I think this treatise a sort of growth from the mind of one who had studied in the Academe, pitying yet loving poor Socrates and his disciples. Yet more, it is the outcome of meditation on that sad history in the Acts, which expounds St. Paul's bitter reminiscences, when he says that his gospel was, "to the Greeks, foolishness." They never "heard him again on this matter." He left them under the confused impressions they had expressed in the *agora*, when they said, "he seemeth to be a setterforth of new gods." St. Luke allows himself a smile only half suppressed when he adds, "because he preached unto them *Jesus and Anastasis*," which in their ears was only a barbarian echo to their own *Phoebus and Artemis;* and what did Athenians want of any more wares of that sort, especially under the introduction of a poor Jew from parts unknown? Did the apostle's prophetic soul foresee Athenagoras, as he "departed from among them"? However that may be, his blessed Master "knew what he would do." He could let none of Paul's words fall to the ground, without taking care that some seeds should bring forth fruit a thousand-fold. Here come the sheaves at last. Athenagoras proves, also, what our Savior meant, when he said to the Galileans, "Ye are the light of the world."

The following is the original Introductory Notice: —

It is one of the most singular facts in early ecclesiastical history, that the name of Athenagoras is scarcely ever mentioned. Only two references to him and his writings have been discovered. One of these occurs in the work of Methodius, *On the Resurrection of the Body*, as preserved by Epiphanius (*Hoer.*, lxiv.) and Photius (*Biblioth.*, ccxxxiv.). The other notice of him is found in the writings of Philip of Side, in

Pamphylia, who flourished in the early part of the fifth century. It is very remarkable that Eusebius should have been altogether silent regarding him; and that writings, so elegant and powerful as are those which still exist under his name, should have been allowed in early times to sink into almost entire oblivion.

We know with certainty regarding Athenagoras, that he was an Athenian philosopher who had embraced Christianity, and that his *Apology*, or, as he styles it, "Embassy" (πρεσβεία), was presented to the Emperors Aurelius and Commodus about a.d. 177. He is supposed to have written a considerable number of works, but the only other production of his extant is his treatise on the Resurrection. It is probable that this work was composed somewhat later than the *Apology* (see chap. xxxvi.), though its exact date cannot be determined. Philip of Side also states that he preceded Pantænus as head of the catechetical school at Alexandria; but this is probably incorrect and is contradicted by Eusebius. A more interesting and perhaps well-rounded statement is made by the same writer respecting Athenagoras, to the effect that he was won over to Christianity while reading the Scriptures in order to controvert them. Both his *Apology* and his treatise on the Resurrection display a practiced pen and a richly cultured mind. He is by far the most elegant, and certainly at the same time one of the ablest, of the early Christian Apologists.

A PLEA FOR THE CHRISTIANS
By Athenagoras the Athenian: Philosopher and Christian

To the Emperors Marcus Aurelius Anoninus and Lucius Aurelius Commodus, conquerors of Armenia and Sarmatia, and more than all, philosophers.

CHAPTER I.—INJUSTICE SHOWN TOWARDS THE CHRISTIANS.

In your empire, greatest of sovereigns, different nations have different customs and laws; and no one is hindered by law or fear of punishment from following his ancestral usages, however ridiculous these may be. A citizen of Ilium calls Hector a god, and pays divine honors to Helen, taking her for Adrasteia. The Lacedæmonian venerates Agamemnon as Zeus, and Phylonoë the daughter of Tyndarus; and the man of Tenedos worships Tennes. The Athenian sacrifices to Erechtheus as Poseidon. The Athenians also perform religious rites and celebrate mysteries in honor of Agraulus and Pandrosus, women who were deemed guilty of impiety for opening the box. In short, among every nation and people, men offer whatever sacrifices and celebrate whatever mysteries they please. The Egyptians reckon among their gods even cats, and crocodiles, and serpents, and asps, and dogs. And to all these both you and the laws give permission so to act, deeming, on the one hand, that to believe in no god at all is impious and wicked, and on the other, that it is necessary for each man to worship the gods he prefers, in order that through fear of the deity, men may be kept from wrong-doing. But why—for do not, like the multitude, be led astray by hearsay—why is a mere name odious to you? Names are not deserving of hatred: it is the unjust act that calls for penalty and punishment. And accordingly, with admiration of your mildness and gentleness, and your peaceful and benevolent disposition towards every man, individuals live in the possession of equal rights; and the cities, according to their rank, share in equal honor; and the whole empire, under your intelligent sway, enjoys profound peace. But for us who are called Christians8 you have not in like manner cared; but although we commit no wrong—nay, as will appear in the sequel of this discourse, are of all men most piously and righteously disposed towards the Deity and towards your government—you allow us to be harassed, plundered, and persecuted, the multitude making war upon us for our name alone. We venture, therefore, to lay a statement of our case before you—and you will team from this discourse that we suffer unjustly, and contrary to all law and reason—and we beseech you to bestow some consideration upon us also, that we may cease at length to be slaughtered at the instigation of false accusers. For the fine imposed by our persecutors does not aim merely at our property, nor their insults at our reputation, nor the damage they do us at any other of our greater interests. These we hold in contempt, though to the generality they appear matters of great importance; for we have learned, not only not to return blow for blow, nor to go to law with those who plunder and rob us, but to those who smite us on one side of the face to offer the other side also, and to those who take away our coat to give likewise our cloak. But, when we have surrendered our property, they plot against our very bodies and souls, pouring upon us wholesale charges of crimes of which we are guiltless even in thought, but which belong to these idle praters themselves, and to the whole tribe of those who are like them.

CHAPTER II. —CLAIM TO BE TREATED AS OTHERS ARE WHEN ACCUSED.

If, indeed, any one can convict us of a crime, be it small or great, we do not ask to be excused from punishment, but are prepared to undergo the sharpest and most merciless inflictions. But if the accusation relates merely to our name—and it is undeniable, that up to the present time the stories told about us rest on nothing better than the common undiscriminating popular talk, nor has any Christian been convicted of crime—it will devolve on you, illustrious and benevolent and most learned sovereigns, to remove by law this despiteful treatment, so that, as throughout the world both individuals and cities partake of your beneficence, we also may feel grateful to you, exulting that we are no longer the victims of false accusation. For it does not comport with your justice, that others when charged with crimes should not be punished till they are convicted, but that in our case the name we bear should have more force than the evidence adduced on the trial, when the judges, instead of inquiring whether the person arraigned have committed any crime, vent their insults on the name, as if that were itself a crime. But no name in and by itself is reckoned either good or bad; names appear bad or good according as the actions underlying them are bad or good. You, however, have yourselves a clear knowledge of this, since you are well instructed in philosophy and all learning. For this reason, too, those who are brought before you for trial, though they may be arraigned on the gravest charges, have no fear, because they know that you will inquire respecting their previous life, and not be influenced by names if they mean nothing, nor by the charges contained in the indictments if they should be false: they accept with equal satisfaction, about its fairness, the sentence whether of condemnation or acquittal. What, therefore, is conceded as the common right of all, we claim for ourselves, that we shall not be hated and punished because we are called Christians (for what has the name to do with our being bad men?), but be tried on any charges which may be brought against us, and either be released on our disproving them, or punished if convicted of crime—not for the name (for no Christian is a bad man unless he falsely profess our doctrines), but for the wrong which has been done. It is thus that we see the philosophers judged. None of them before trial is deemed by the judge either good or bad because of his science or art, but if found guilty of wickedness he is punished, without thereby affixing any stigma on philosophy (for he is a bad man for not cultivating philosophy in a lawful manner, but science is blameless), while if he refutes the false charges he is acquitted. Let this equal justice, then, be done to us. Let the life of the accused persons be investigated, but let the name stand free from all imputation. I must at the outset of my defense entreat you, illustrious emperors, to listen to me impartially: not to be carried away by the common irrational talk and prejudge the case, but to apply your desire of knowledge and love of truth to the examination of our doctrine also. Thus, while you on your part will not err through ignorance, we also, by disproving the charges arising out of the undiscerning rumor of the multitude, shall cease to be assailed.

CHAPTER III. —CHARGES BROUGHT AGAINST THE CHRISTIANS.

Three things are alleged against us: atheism, Thyestean feasts, OEdipodean intercourse. But if these charges are true, spare no class: proceed at once against our crimes; destroy us root and branch, with our wives and children, if any Christian is found to live like the brutes. And yet even the brutes do not touch the flesh of their own kind; and they pair by a law of nature, and only at the regular season, not from simple wantonness; they also recognize those from whom they receive benefits. If any one, therefore, is more savage than the brutes, what punishment that he can endure shall be deemed adequate to such offences? But, if these things are only idle tales and empty slanders, originating in the fact that virtue is opposed by its very nature to vice, and that contraries war against one another by a divine law (and you are yourselves witnesses that no such iniquities are committed by us, for you forbid informations to be laid against us), it remains for you to make inquiry concerning our life, our opinions, our loyalty and obedience to you and your house and government, and thus at length to grant to us the same rights (we ask nothing more) as to those who persecute us. For we shall then conquer them, unhesitatingly surrendering, as we now do, our very lives for the truth's sake.

CHAPTER IV. —THE CHRISTIANS ARE NOT ATHEISTS, BUT ACKNOWLEDGE ONE ONLY GOD.

As regards, first of all, the allegation that we are atheists—for I will meet the charges one by one, that we may not be ridiculed for having no answer to give to those who make them—with reason did the Athenians adjudge Diagoras guilty of atheism, in that he not only divulged the Orphic doctrine, and published the mysteries of Eleusis and of the Cabiri, and chopped up the wooden statue of Hercules to boil his turnips, but openly declared that there was no God at all. But to us, who distinguish God from matter, and teach that matter is one thing and God another, and that they are separated by a wide interval (for that the Deity is uncreated and eternal, to be beheld by the understanding and reason alone, while matter is created and perishable), is it not absurd to apply the name of atheism? If our sentiments were like those of Diagoras, while we have such incentives to piety—in the established order, the universal harmony, the magnitude, the color, the form, the arrangement of the world—with reason might our reputation for impiety, as well as the cause of our being thus harassed, be charged on ourselves. But, since our doctrine acknowledges one God, the Maker of this universe, who is Himself uncreated (for that which is does not come to be, but that which is not) but has made all things by the Logos which is from Him, we are treated unreasonably in both respects, in that we are both defamed and persecuted.

CHAPTER V.—TESTIMONY OF THE POETS TO THE UNITY OF GOD.

Poets and philosophers have not been voted atheists for inquiring concerning God. Euripides, speaking of those who, according to popular preconception, are ignorantly called gods, says doubtingly: —

"If Zeus indeed does reign in heaven above,
He ought not on the righteous ills to send."

But speaking of Him who is apprehended by the understanding as matter of certain knowledge, he gives his opinion decidedly, and with intelligence, thus: —

"Seest thou on high him who, with humid arms,
Clasps both the boundless ether and the earth?
Him reckon Zeus, and him regard as God."

For, as to these so-called gods, he neither saw any real existences, to which a name is usually assigned, underlying them ("Zeus," for instance: "who Zeus is I know not, but by report"), nor that any names were given to realities which actually do exist (for of what use are names to those who have no real existences underlying them?); but Him he did see by means of His works, considering with an eye to things unseen the things which are manifest in air, in ether, on earth. Him therefore, from whom proceed all created things, and by whose Spirit they are governed, he concluded to be God; and Sophocles agrees with him, when he says: —

"There is one God, in truth there is but one,
Who made the heavens, and the broad earth beneath."

[Euripides is speaking] of the nature of God, which fills His works with beauty, and teaching both where God must be, and that He must be One.

CHAPTER VI. —OPINIONS OF THE PHILOSOPHERS AS TO THE ONE GOD.

Philolaus, too, when he says that all things are included in God as in a stronghold, teaches that He is one, and that He is superior to matter. Lysis and Opsimus thus define God: the one says that He is an ineffable number, the other that He is the excess of the greatest number beyond that which comes nearest to it. So that since ten is the greatest number according to the Pythagoreans, being the Tetractys, and containing all the arithmetic and harmonic principles, and the Nine stands next to it, God is a unit—that is, one. For the greatest number exceeds the next least by one. Then there are Plato and Aristotle—not that I am about to go through all that the philosophers have said about God, as if I wished to exhibit a complete summary of their opinions; for I know that, as you excel all men in intelligence and in the power of your rule, in the same proportion do you surpass them all in an accurate acquaintance with all learning, cultivating as you do each several branch with more success than even those who have devoted themselves exclusively to any one. But, since it is impossible to demonstrate without the citation of names that we are not alone in confining the notion of God to unity, I have ventured on an enumeration of opinions. Plato, then, says, "To find out the Maker and Father of this universe is difficult; and, when found, it is impossible to declare Him to all," conceiving of one uncreated and eternal God. And if he recognizes others as well, such as the sun, moon, and stars, yet he recognizes them as created: "gods, offspring of gods, of whom I am the Maker, and the Father of works which are indissoluble apart from my will; but whatever is compounded can be dissolved." If, therefore, Plato is not an atheist for conceiving of one uncreated God, the Framer of the universe, neither are we atheists who acknowledge and firmly hold that He is God who has framed all things by the Logos and holds them in being by His Spirit. Aristotle, again, and his followers, recognizing the existence of one whom they regard as a sort of compound living creature (ζῷον), speak of God as consisting of soul and body, thinking His body to be the etherial space and the planetary stars and the sphere of the fixed stars, moving in circles; but His soul, the reason which presides over the motion of the body, itself not subject to motion, but becoming the cause of motion to the other. The Stoics also, although by the appellations they employ to suit the changes of matter, which they say is permeated by the Spirit of God, they multiply the Deity in name, yet in reality they consider God to be one. For, if God is an artistic fire advancing methodically to the production of the several things in the world, embracing in Himself all the seminal principles by which each thing is produced in accordance with fate, and if His Spirit pervades the whole world, then God is one according to them, being named Zeus in respect of the fervid part (τὸ ζέον) of matter, and Hera in respect of the air (ὁ ἀήρ), and called by other names in respect of that particular part of matter which He pervades.

CHAPTER VII. —SUPERIORITY OF THE CHRISTIAN DOCTRINE RESPECTING GOD.

Since, therefore, the unity of the Deity is confessed by almost all, even against their will, when they come to treat of the first principles of the universe, and we in our turn likewise assert that He who arranged this universe is God,—why is it that they can say and write with impunity what they please concerning the Deity, but that against us a law lies in force, though we are able to demonstrate what we apprehend and justly believe, namely that there is one God, with proofs and reason accordant with truth? For poets and philosophers, as to other subjects so also to this, have applied themselves in the way of conjecture, moved, by reason of their affinity with the afflatus from God, each one by his own soul, to try whether he could find out and apprehend the truth; but they have not been found competent fully to apprehend it, because they thought fit to learn, not from God concerning God, but each one from himself; hence they came each to his own conclusion respecting God, and matter, and forms, and the world. But we have for witnesses of the things we apprehend and believe, prophets, men who have pronounced concerning God and the things of God, guided by the Spirit of God. And you too will admit, excelling all others as you do in intelligence and in piety towards the true God (τὸ ὄντως θεῖον), that it would be irrational for us to cease to believe in the Spirit from God, who moved the mouths of the prophets like musical instruments, and to give heed to mere human opinions.

CHAPTER VIII. —ABSURDITIES OF POLYTHEISM.

About, then, the doctrine that there was from the beginning one God, the Maker of this universe, consider it in this wise, that you may be acquainted with the argumentative grounds also of our faith. If there were from the beginning two or more gods, they were either in one and the same place, or each of them separately in his own. In one and the same place they could not be. For, if they are gods, they are not alike; but because they are uncreated they are unlike: for created things are like their patterns; but the uncreated are unlike, being neither produced from any one, nor formed after the pattern of any one. Hand and eye and foot are parts of one body, making up together one man: is God in this sense one? And indeed Socrates was compounded and divided into parts, just because he was created and perishable; but God is uncreated, and, impassible, and indivisible—does not, therefore, consist of parts. But if, on the contrary, each of them exists separately, since He that made the world is above the things created, and about the things He has made and set in order, where can the other or the rest be? For if the world, being made spherical, is confined within the circles of heaven, and the Creator of the world is above the things created, managing that by His providential care of these, what place is there for the second god, or for the other gods? For he is not in the world, because it belongs to the other; nor about the world, for God the Maker of the world is above it. But if he is neither in the world nor about the world (for all that surrounds it is occupied by this one), where is he? Is he above the world and [the first] God? In another world, or about another? But if he is in another or about another, then he is not about us, for he does not govern the world; nor is his power great, for he exists in a circumscribed space. But if he is neither in another world (for all things are filled by the other), nor about another (for all things are occupied by the other), he clearly does not exist at all, for there is no place in which he can be. Or what does he do, seeing there is another to whom the world belongs, and he is above the Maker of the world, and yet is neither in the world nor about the world? Is there, then, some other place where he can stand? But God, and what belongs to God, are above him. And what, too, shall be the place, seeing that the other fills the regions which are above the world? Perhaps he exerts a providential care? [By no means.] And yet, unless he does so, he has done nothing. If, then, he neither does anything nor exercises providential care, and if there is not another place in which he is, then this Being of whom we speak is the one God from the beginning, and the sole Maker of the world.

CHAPTER IX. —THE TESTIMONY OF THE PROPHETS.

If we satisfied ourselves with advancing such considerations as these, our doctrines might by some be looked upon as human. But, since the voices of the prophets confirm our arguments—for I think that you also, with your great zeal for knowledge, and your great attainments in learning, cannot be ignorant of the writings either of Moses or of Isaiah and Jeremiah, and the other prophets, who, lifted in ecstasy above the natural operations of their minds by the impulses of the Divine Spirit, uttered the things with which they were inspired, the Spirit making use of them as a flute-player breathes into a flute; —what, then, do these men say? "The Lord is our God; no other can be compared with Him." And again: "I am God, the first and the last, and besides Me there is no God." In like manner: "Before Me there was no other God, and after Me there shall be none; I am God, and there is none besides Me." And as to His greatness: "Heaven is My throne, and the earth is the footstool of My feet: what house will ye build for Me, or what is the place of My rest?" But I leave it to you, when you meet with the books themselves, to examine carefully the prophecies contained in them, that you may on fitting grounds defend us from the abuse cast upon us.

CHAPTER X.—THE CHRISTIANS WORSHIP THE FATHER, SON, AND HOLY GHOST.

That we are not atheists, therefore, seeing that we acknowledge one God, uncreated, eternal, invisible, impassible, incomprehensible, illimitable, who is apprehended by the understanding only and the reason, who is encompassed by light, and beauty, and spirit, and power ineffable, by whom the universe has been created through His Logos, and set in order, and is kept in being—I have sufficiently demonstrated. [I say "His Logos"], for we acknowledge also a Son of God. Nor let any one think it ridiculous that God should have a Son. For though the poets, in their fictions, represent the gods as no better than men, our mode of thinking is not the same as theirs, concerning either God the Father or the Son. But the Son of God is the Logos of the Father, in idea and in operation; for after the pattern of Him and by Him were all things made, the Father and the Son being one. And, the Son being in the Father and the Father in the Son, in oneness and power of spirit, the understanding and reason (νοῦς καὶ λόγος) of the Father is the Son of God. But if, in your surpassing intelligence, it occurs to you to inquire what is meant by the Son, I will state briefly that He is the first product of the Father, not as having been brought into existence (for from the beginning, God, who is the eternal mind [νοῦς], had the Logos in Himself, being from eternity instinct with Logos [λογικός]); but inasmuch as He came forth to be the idea and energizing power of all material things, which lay like a nature without attributes, and an inactive earth, the grosser particles being mixed up with the lighter. The prophetic Spirit also agrees with our statements. "The Lord," it says, "made me, the beginning of His ways to His works." The Holy Spirit Himself also, which operates in the prophets, we assert to be an effluence of God, flowing from Him, and returning back again like a beam of the sun. Who, then, would not be astonished to hear men who speak of God the Father, and of God the Son, and of the Holy Spirit, and who declare both their power in union and their distinction in order, called atheists? Nor is our teaching in what relates to the divine nature confined to these points; but we recognize also a multitude of angels and ministers, whom God the Maker and Framer of the world distributed and appointed to their several posts by His Logos, to occupy themselves about the elements, and the heavens, and the world, and the things in it, and the goodly ordering of them all.

CHAPTER XI. —THE MORAL TEACHING OF THE CHRISTIANS REPELS THE CHARGE BROUGHT AGAINST THEM.

If I go minutely into the particulars of our doctrine, let it not surprise you. It is that you may not be carried away by the popular and irrational opinion but may have the truth clearly before you. For presenting the opinions themselves to which we adhere, as being not human but uttered and taught by God, we shall be able to persuade you not to think of us as atheists. What, then, are those teachings in which we are brought up? "I say unto you, Love your enemies; bless them that curse you; pray for them that persecute you; that ye may be the sons of your Father who is in heaven, who causes His sun to rise on the evil and the good, and sends rain on the just and the unjust." Allow me here to lift up my voice boldly in loud and audible outcry, pleading as I do before philosophic princes. For who of those that reduce syllogisms, and clear up ambiguities, and explain etymologies, or of those who teach homonyms and synonyms, and predicaments and axioms, and what is the subject and what the predicate, and who promise their disciples by these and such like instructions to make them happy: who of them have so purged their souls as, instead of hating their enemies, to love them; and, instead of speaking ill of those who have reviled them (to abstain from which is of itself an evidence of no mean forbearance), to bless them; and to pray for those who plot against their lives? On the contrary, they never cease with evil intent to search out skilfully the secrets of their art, and are ever bent on working some ill, making the art of words and not the exhibition of deeds their business and profession. But among us you will find uneducated persons, and artisans, and old women, who, if they are unable in words to prove the benefit of our doctrine, yet by their deeds exhibit the benefit arising from their persuasion of its truth: they do not rehearse speeches, but exhibit good works; when struck, they do not strike again; when robbed, they do not go to law; they give to those that ask of them, and love their neighbors as themselves.

CHAPTER XII. —CONSEQUENT ABSURDITY OF THE CHARGE OF ATHEISM.

Should we, then, unless we believed that a God presides over the human race, thus purge ourselves from evil? Most certainly not. But, because we are persuaded that we shall give an account of everything in the present life to God, who made us and the world, we adopt a temperate and benevolent and generally despised method of life, believing that we shall suffer no such great evil here, even should our lives be taken from us, compared with what we shall there receive for our meek and benevolent and moderate life from the great Judge. Plato indeed has said that Minos and Rhadamanthus will judge and punish the wicked; but we say that, even if a man be Minos or Rhadamanthus himself, or their father, even he will not escape the judgment of God. Are, then, those who consider life to be comprised in this, "Let us eat and drink, for to-morrow we die," and who regard death as a deep sleep and forgetfulness ("sleep and death, twin brothers"), to be accounted pious; while men who reckon the present life of very small worth indeed, and who are conducted to the future life by this one thing alone, that they know God and His Logos, what is the oneness of the Son with the Father, what the communion of the Father with the Son, what is the Spirit, what is the unity of these three, the Spirit, the Son, the Father, and their distinction in unity; and who know that the life for which we look is far better than can be described in words, provided we arrive at it pure from all wrong-doing; who, moreover, carry our benevolence to such an extent, that we not only love our friends ("for if ye love them," He says, "that love you, and lend to them that lend to you, what reward will ye have?"),—shall we, I say, when such is our character, and when we live such a life as this, that we may escape condemnation at last, not be accounted pious? These, however, are only small matters taken from great, and a few things from many, that we may not further trespass on your patience; for those who test honey and whey, judge by a small quantity whether the whole is good.

CHAPTER XIII. —WHY THE CHRISTIANS DO NOT OFFER SACRIFICES.

But, as most of those who charge us with atheism, and that because they have not even the dreamiest conception of what God is and are doltish and utterly unacquainted with natural and divine things, and such as measure piety by the rule of sacrifices, charges us with not acknowledging the same gods as the cities, be pleased to attend to the following considerations, O emperors, on both points. And first, as to our not sacrificing: the Framer and Father of this universe does not need blood, nor the odor of burnt-offerings, nor the fragrance of flowers and incense, forasmuch as He is Himself perfect fragrance, needing nothing either within or without; but the noblest sacrifice to Him is for us to know who stretched out and vaulted the heavens, and fixed the earth in its place like a centre, who gathered the water into seas and divided the light from the darkness, who adorned the sky with stars and made the earth to bring forth seed of every kind, who made animals and fashioned man. When, holding God to be this Framer of all things, who preserves them in being and superintends them all by knowledge and administrative skill, we "lift up holy hands" to Him, what need has He further of a hecatomb? "For they, when mortals have transgressed or failed to do aright, by sacrifice and prayer, Libations and burnt-offerings, may be soothed." And what have I to do with holocausts, which God does not stand in need of? —though indeed it does behoove us to offer a bloodless sacrifice and "the service of our reason."

CHAPTER XIV. —INCONSISTENCY OF THOSE WHO ACCUSE THE CHRISTIANS.

Then, as to the other complaint, that we do not pray to and believe in the same gods as the cities, it is an exceedingly silly one. Why, the very men who charge us with atheism for not admitting the same gods as they acknowledge, are not agreed among themselves concerning the gods. The Athenians have set up as gods Celeus and Metanira: the Lacedæmonians Menelaus; and they offer sacrifices and hold festivals to him, while the men of Ilium cannot endure the very sound of his name and pay their adoration to Hector. The Ceans worship Aristæus, considering him to be the same as Zeus and Apollo; the Thasians Theagenes, a man who committed murder at the Olympic games; the Samians Lysander, notwithstanding all the slaughters and all the crimes perpetrated by him; Alcman and Hesiod Medea, and the Cilicians Niobe; the Sicilians Philip the son of Butacides; the Amathusians Onesilus; the Carthaginians Hamilcar. Time would fail me to enumerate the whole. When, therefore, they differ among themselves concerning their gods, why do they bring the charge against us of not agreeing with them? Then look at the practices prevailing among the Egyptians: are they not perfectly ridiculous? For in the temples at their solemn festivals they beat their breasts as for the dead, and sacrifice to the same beings as gods; and no wonder, when they look upon the brutes as gods, and shave themselves when they die, and bury them in temples, and make public lamentation. If, then, we are guilty of impiety because we do not practice a piety corresponding with theirs, then all cities and all nations are guilty of impiety, for they do not all acknowledge the same gods.

CHAPTER XV. —THE CHRISTIANS DISTINGUISH GOD FROM MATTER.

But grant that they acknowledge the same. What then? Because the multitude, who cannot distinguish between matter and God, or see how great is the interval which lies between them, pray to idols made of matter, are we therefore, who do distinguish and separate the uncreated and the created, that which is and that which is not, that which is apprehended by the understanding and that which is perceived by the senses, and who give the fitting name to each of them,—are we to come and worship images? If, indeed, matter and God are the same, two names for one thing, then certainly, in not regarding stocks and stones, gold and silver, as gods, we are guilty of impiety. But if they are at the greatest possible remove from one another—as far asunder as the artist and the materials of his art—why are we called to account? For as is the potter and the clay (matter being the clay, and the artist the potter), so is God, the Framer of the world, and matter, which is subservient to Him for the purposes of His art. But as the clay cannot become vessels of itself without art, so neither did matter, which can take all forms, receive, apart from God the Framer, distinction and shape and order. And as we do not hold the pottery of more worth than him who made it, nor the vessels of glass and gold than him who wrought them; but if there is anything about them elegant in art we praise the artificer, and it is he who reaps the glory of the vessels: even so with matter and God—the glory and honor of the orderly arrangement of the world belongs of right not to matter, but to God, the Framer of matter. So that, if we were to regard the various forms of matter as gods, we should seem to be without any sense of the true God, because we should be putting the things which are dissoluble and perishable on a level with that which is eternal.

CHAPTER XVI. —THE CHRISTIANS DO NOT WORSHIP THE UNIVERSE.

Beautiful without doubt is the world, excelling, as well in its magnitude as in the arrangement of its parts, both those in the oblique circle and those about the north, and also in its spherical form. Yet it is not this, but its Artificer, that we must worship. For when any of your subjects come to you, they do not neglect to pay their homage to you, their rulers and lords, from whom they will obtain whatever they need, and address themselves to the magnificence of your palace; but, if they chance to come upon the royal residence, they bestow a passing glance of admiration on its beautiful structure: but it is to you yourselves that they show honor, as being "all in all." You sovereigns, indeed, rear and adorn your palaces for yourselves; but the world was not created because God needed it; for God is Himself everything to Himself, —light unapproachable, a perfect world, spirit, power, reason. If, therefore, the world is an instrument in tune, and moving in well-measured time, I adore the Being who gave its harmony, and strikes its notes, and sings the accordant strain, and not the instrument. For at the musical contests the adjudicators do not pass by the lute players and crown the lutes. Whether, then, as Plato says, the world be a product of divine art, I admire its beauty, and adore the Artificer; or whether it be His essence and body, as the Peripatetics affirm, we do not neglect to adore God, who is the cause of the motion of the body, and descend "to the poor and weak elements," adoring in the impassible air (as they term it), passible matter; or, if any one apprehends the several parts of the world to be powers of God, we do not approach and do homage to the powers, but their Maker and Lord. I do not ask of matter what it has not to give, nor passing God by do I pay homage to the elements, which can do nothing more than what they were bidden; for, although they are beautiful to look upon, by reason of the art of their Framer, yet they still have the nature of matter. And to this view Plato also bears testimony; "for," says he, "that which is called heaven and earth has received many blessings from the Father, but yet partakes of body; hence it cannot possibly be free from change." If, therefore, while I admire the heavens and the elements in respect of their art, I do not worship them as gods, knowing that the law of dissolution is upon them, how can I call those objects gods of which I know the makers to be men? Attend, I beg, to a few words on this subject.

CHAPTER XVII. —THE NAMES OF THE GODS AND THEIR IMAGES ARE BUT OF RECENT DATE.

An apologist must adduce more precise arguments than I have yet given, both concerning the names of the gods, to show that they are of recent origin, and concerning their images, to show that they are, so to say, but of yesterday. You yourselves, however, are thoroughly acquainted with these matters, since you are versed in all departments of knowledge, and are beyond all other men familiar with the ancients. I assert, then, that it was Orpheus, and Homer, and Hesiod who gave both genealogies and names to those whom they call gods. Such, too, is the testimony of Herodotus. "My opinion," he says, "is that Hesiod and Homer preceded me by four hundred years, and no more; and it was they who framed a theogony for the Greeks, and gave the gods their names, and assigned them their several honors and functions, and described their forms." Representations of the gods, again, were not in use at all, so long as statuary, and painting, and sculpture were unknown; nor did they become common until Saurias the Samian, and Crato the Sicyonian, and Cleanthes the Corinthian, and the Corinthian damsel appeared, when drawing in outline was invented by Saurias, who sketched a horse in the sun, and painting by Crato, who painted in oil on a whitened tablet the outlines of a man and woman; and the art of making figures in relief (κοροπλαθική) was invented by the damsel, who, being in love with a person, traced his shadow on a wall as he lay asleep, and her father, being delighted with the exactness of the resemblance (he was a potter), carved out the sketch and filled it up with clay: this figure is still preserved at Corinth. After these, Dædalus and Theodorus the Milesian further invented sculpture and statuary. You perceive, then, that the time since representations of form and the making of images began is so short, that we can name the artist of each particular god. The image of Artemis at Ephesus, for example, and that of Athenâ (or rather of Athelâ, for so is she named by those who speak more in the style of the mysteries; for thus was the ancient image made of the olive-tree called), and the sitting figure of the same goddess, were made by Endoeus, a pupil of Dædalus; the Pythian god was the work of Theodorus and Telecles; and the Delian god and Artemis are due to the art of Tectæus and Angelio; Hera in Samos and in Argos came from the hands of Smilis, and the other statues were by Phidias; Aphrodité the courtezan in Cnidus is the production of Praxiteles; Asclepius in Epidaurus is the work of Phidias. In a word, of not one of these statues can it be said that it was not made by man. If, then, these are gods, why did they not exist from the beginning? Why, in sooth, are they younger than those who made them? Why, in sooth, in order to their coming into existence, did they need the aid of men and art? They are nothing but earth, and stones, and matter, and curious art.

CHAPTER XVIII. —THE GODS THEMSELVES HAVE BEEN CREATED, AS THE POETS CONFESS.

But, since it is affirmed by some that, although these are only images, yet there exist gods in honor of whom they are made; and that the supplications and sacrifices presented to the images are to be referred to the gods, and are in fact made to the gods; and that there is not any other way of coming to them, for

> "'Tis hard for man
> To meet in presence visible a God;"

and whereas, in proof that such is the fact, they adduce the energies possessed by certain images, let us examine into the power attached to their names. And I would beseech you, greatest of emperors, before I enter on this discussion, to be indulgent to me while I bring forward true considerations; for it is not my design to show the fallacy of idols, but, by disproving the calumnies vented against us, to offer a reason for the course of life we follow.

May you, by considering yourselves, be able to discover the heavenly kingdom also! For as all things are subservient to you, father and son, who have received the kingdom from above (for "the king's soul is in the hand of God," saith the prophetic Spirit), so to the one God and the Logos proceeding from Him, the Son, apprehended by us as inseparable from Him, all things are in like manner subjected. This then especially I beg you carefully to consider. The gods, as they affirm, were not from the beginning, but every one of them has come into existence just like ourselves. And in this opinion, they all agree. Homer speaks of

> "Old Oceanus,
> The sire of gods, and Tethys;"

and Orpheus (who, moreover, was the first to invent their names, and recounted their births, and narrated the exploits of each, and is believed by them to treat with greater truth than others of divine things, whom Homer himself follows in most matters, especially about the gods)—he, too, has fixed their first origin to be from water: —

> "Oceanus, the origin of all."

For, according to him, water was the beginning of all things, and from water mud was formed, and from both was produced an animal, a dragon with the head of a lion growing to it, and between the two heads there was the face of a god, named Heracles and Kronos. This Heracles generated an egg of enormous size, which, on becoming full, was, by the powerful friction of its generator, burst into two, the part at the top receiving the form of heaven (οὐρανός), and the lower part that of earth (γῆ). The goddess Gê moreover, came forth with a body; and Ouranos, by his union with Gê, begat females, Clotho, Lachesis, and Atropos; and males, the hundred-handed Cottys, Gyges, Briareus, and the Cyclopes Brontes, and Steropes, and Argos, whom also he bound and hurled down to

Tartarus, having learnt that he was to be ejected from his government by his children; whereupon Gê, being enraged, brought forth the Titans.

> "The godlike Gaia bore to Ouranos
> Sons who are by the name of Titans known,
> Because they vengeance took on Ouranos,
> Majestic, glitt'ring with his starry crown."

CHAPTER XIX. —THE PHILOSOPHERS AGREE WITH THE POETS RESPECTING THE GODS.

Such was the beginning of the existence both of their gods and of the universe. Now what are we to make of this? For each of those things to which divinity is ascribed is conceived of as having existed from the first. For, if they have come into being, having previously had no existence, as those say who treat of the gods, they do not exist. For, a thing is either uncreated and eternal, or created and perishable. Nor do I think one thing and the philosophers another. "What is that which always is, and has no origin; or what is that which has been originated, yet never is?" Discoursing of the intelligible and the sensible, Plato teaches that that which always is, the intelligible, is unoriginated, but that which is not, the sensible, is originated, beginning to be and ceasing to exist. In like manner, the Stoics also say that all things will be burnt up and will again exist, the world receiving another beginning. But if, although there is, according to them, a twofold cause, one active and governing, namely providence, the other passive and changeable, namely matter, it is nevertheless impossible for the world, even though under the care of Providence, to remain in the same state, because it is created—how can the constitution of these gods remain, who are not self-existent, but have been originated? And in what are the gods superior to matter, since they derive their constitution from water? But not even water, according to them, is the beginning of all things. From simple and homogeneous elements what could be constituted?

Moreover, matter requires an artificer, and the artificer requires matter. For how could figures be made without matter or an artificer? Neither, again, is it reasonable that matter should be older than God; for the efficient cause must of necessity exist before the things that are made.

CHAPTER XX. —ABSURD REPRESENTATIONS OF THE GODS.

If the absurdity of their theology were confined to saying that the gods were created, and owed their constitution to water, since I have demonstrated that nothing is made which is not also liable to dissolution, I might proceed to the remaining charges. But, on the one hand, they have described their bodily forms: speaking of Hercules, for instance, as a god in the shape of a dragon coiled up; of others as hundred-handed; of the daughter of Zeus, whom he begat of his mother Rhea; or of Demeter, as having two eyes in the natural order, and two in her forehead, and the face of an animal on the back part of her neck, and as having also horns, so that Rhea, frightened at her monster of a child, fled from her, and did not give her the breast (θηλή), whence mystically she is called Athêlâ, but commonly Phersephoné and Koré, though she is not the same as Athênâ, who is called Koré from the pupil of the eye;—and, on the other hand, they have described their admirable achievements, as they deem them: how Kronos, for instance, mutilated his father, and hurled him down from his chariot, and how he murdered his children, and swallowed the males of them; and how Zeus bound his father, and cast him down to Tartarus, as did Ouranos also to his sons, and fought with the Titans for the government; and how he persecuted his mother Rhea when she refused to wed him, and, she becoming a she-dragon, and he himself being changed into a dragon, bound her with what is called the Herculean knot, and accomplished his purpose, of which fact the rod of Hermes is a symbol; and again, how he violated his daughter Phersephoné, in this case also assuming the form of a dragon, and became the father of Dionysus. In face of narrations like these, I must say at least this much, What that is becoming or useful is there in such a history, that we must believe Kronos, Zeus, Koré, and the rest, to be gods? Is it the descriptions of their bodies? Why, what man of judgment and reflection will believe that a viper was begotten by a god (thus Orpheus: —

> "But from the sacred womb Phanes begat
> Another offspring, horrible and fierce,
> In sight a frightful viper, on whose head
> Were hairs: its face was comely; but the rest,
> From the neck downwards, bore the aspect dire
> Of a dread dragon");

or who will admit that Phanes himself, being a first-born god (for he it was that was produced from the egg), has the body or shape of a dragon, or was swallowed by Zeus, that Zeus might be too large to be contained? For if they differ in no respect from the lowest brutes (since it is evident that the Deity must differ from the things of earth and those that are derived from matter), they are not gods. How, then, I ask, can we approach them as suppliants, when their origin resembles that of cattle, and they themselves have the form of brutes, and are ugly to behold?

CHAPTER XXI. —IMPURE LOVES ASCRIBED TO THE GODS.

But should it be said that they only had fleshly forms, and possess blood and seed, and the affections of anger and sexual desire, even then we must regard such assertions as nonsensical and ridiculous; for there is neither anger, nor desire and appetite, nor procreative seed, in gods. Let them, then, have fleshly forms, but let them be superior to wrath and anger, that Athênâ may not be seen

> "Burning with rage and inly wroth with Jove;"

nor Hera appear thus: —

> "Juno's breast
> Could not contain her rage."

And let them be superior to grief: —

> "A woful sight mine eyes behold: a man
> I love in flight around the walls! My heart
> For Hector grieves."

For I call even men rude and stupid who give way to anger and grief. But when the "father of men and gods" mourns for his son, —

> "Woe, woe! that fate decrees my best belov'd
> Sarpedon, by Patroclus' hand to fall;"

and is not able while he mourns to rescue him from his peril: —

> "The son of Jove, yet Jove preserv'd him not;"

who would not blame the folly of those who, with tales like these, are lovers of the gods, or rather, live without any god? Let them have fleshly forms, but let not Aphrodité be wounded by Diomedes in her body: —

> "The haughty son of Tydeus, Diomed,
> Hath wounded me;"

or by Arês in her soul: —

> "Me, awkward me, she scorns; and yields her charms
> To that fair lecher, the strong god of arms."
> "The weapon pierced the flesh."

He who was terrible in battle, the ally of Zeus against the Titans, is shown to be weaker than Diomedes: —

"He raged, as Mars, when brandishing his spear."
Hush! Homer, a god never rages. But you describe the god to me as blood-stained, and the bane of mortals: —

"Mars, Mars, the bane of mortals, stained with blood;"

and you tell of his adultery and his bonds: —

> "Then, nothing loth, th' enamour'd fair he led,
> And sunk transported on the conscious bed.
> Down rushed the toils."

Do they not pour forth impious stuff of this sort in abundance concerning the gods? Ouranos is mutilated; Kronos is bound, and thrust down to Tartarus; the Titans revolt; Styx dies in battle: yea, they even represent them as mortal; they are in love with one another; they are in love with human beings: —

> "Æneas, amid Ida's jutting peaks,
> Immortal Venus to Anchises bore."

Are they not in love? Do they not suffer? Nay, verily, they are gods, and desire cannot touch them! Even though a god assume flesh in pursuance of a divine purpose, he is therefore the slave of desire.

> "For never yet did such a flood of love,
> For goddess or for mortal, fill my soul;
> Not for Ixion's beauteous wife, who bore
> Pirithöus, sage in council as the gods;
> Nor the neat-footed maiden Danäe,
> A crisius' daughter, her who Perséus bore,
> Th' observ'd of all; nor noble Phoenix' child;
> . . . . . . nor for Semele;
> Nor for Alcmena fair; . . .
> No, nor for Ceres, golden-tressèd queen;
> Nor for Latona bright; nor for thyself."

He is created, he is perishable, with no trace of a god in him. Nay, they are even the hired servants of men: —

> "Admetus' halls, in which I have endured
> To praise the menial table, though a god."

And they tend cattle: —

> "And coming to this land, I cattle fed,
> For him that was my host, and kept this house."

Admetus, therefore, was superior to the god. prophet and wise one, and who canst foresee for others the things that shall be, thou didst not divine the slaughter of thy beloved, but didst even kill him with thine own hand, dear as he was: —

> "And I believed Apollo's mouth divine
> Was full of truth, as well as prophet's art."

(Æschylus is reproaching Apollo for being a false prophet:)—

> "The very one who sings while at the feast,
> The one who said these things, alas! is he
> Who slew my son."

CHAPTER XXII. —PRETENDED SYMBOLICAL EXPLANATIONS.

But perhaps these things are poetic vagary, and there is some natural explanation of them, such as this by Empedocles: —

> "Let Jove be fire, and Juno source of life,
> With Pluto and Nêstis, who bathes with tears
> The human founts."

If, then, Zeus is fire, and Hera the earth, and Aïdoneus the air, and Nê stis water, and these are elements—fire, water, air—

none of them is a god, neither Zeus, nor Hera, nor Aïdoneus; for from matter separated into parts by God is their constitution and origin: —

"Fire, water, earth, and the air's gentle height,
And harmony with these."

Here are things which without harmony cannot abide; which would be brought to ruin by strife: how then can any one says that they are gods? Friendship, according to Empedocles, has an aptitude to govern, things that are compounded are governed, and that which is apt to govern has the dominion; so that if we make the power of the governed and the governing one and the same, we shall be, unawares to ourselves, putting perishable and fluctuating and changeable matter on an equality with the uncreated, and eternal, and ever self-accordant God. Zeus is, according to the Stoics, the fervid part of nature; Hera is the air (ἀήρ)—the very name, if it be joined to itself, signifying this; Poseidon is what is drunk (water, πόσις). But these things are by different persons explained of natural objects in different ways. Some call Zeus twofold masculine-feminine air; others the season which brings about mild weather, on which account it was that he alone escaped from Kronos. But to the Stoics it may be said, If you acknowledge one God, the supreme and uncreated and eternal One, and as many compound bodies as there are changes of matter, and say that the Spirit of God, which pervades matter, obtains according to its variations a diversity of names, the forms of matter will become the body of God; but when the elements are destroyed in the conflagration, the names will necessarily perish along with the forms, the Spirit of God alone remaining. Who, then, can believe that those bodies, of which the variation according to matter is allied to corruption, are gods? But to those who say that Kronos is time, and Rhea the earth, and that she becomes pregnant by Kronos, and brings forth, whence she is regarded as the mother of all; and that he begets and devours his offspring; and that the mutilation is the intercourse of the male with the female, which cuts off the seed and casts it into the womb, and generates a human being, who has in himself the sexual desire, which is Aphrodité; and that the madness of Kronos is the turn of season, which destroys animate and inanimate things; and that the bonds and Tartarus are time, which is changed by seasons and disappears;—to such persons we say, If Kronos is time, he changes; if a season, he turns about; if darkness, or frost, or the moist part of nature, none of these is abiding; but the Deity is immortal, and immoveable, and unalterable: so that neither is Kronos nor his image God. About Zeus again: If he is air, born of Kronos, of which the male part is called Zeus and the female Hera (whence both sister and wife), he is subject to change; if a season, he turns about: but the Deity neither changes nor shifts about. But why should I trespass on your patience by saying more, when you know so well what has been said by each of those who have resolved these things into nature, or what various writers have thought concerning nature, or what they say concerning Athênâ, whom they affirm to be the wisdom (φρόνησις) pervading all things; and concerning Isis, whom they call the birth of all time (φύσις αἰῶνος), from whom all have sprung, and by whom all exist; or concerning Osiris, on whose murder by Typhon his brother Isis with her son Orus sought after his limbs, and finding them honored them with a sepulcher, which sepulcher is to this day called the tomb of Osiris? For whilst they wander up and down about the forms of matter, they miss to find the God who can only be beheld by the reason, while they deify the elements and their several parts, applying different names to them at different times: calling the sowing of the corn, for instance, Osiris (hence they say, that in the mysteries, on the finding of the members of his body, or the fruits, Isis is thus addressed: We have found, we wish thee joy), the fruit of the vine Dionysus, the vine itself Semelé, the heat of the sun the thunderbolt. And yet, in fact, they who refer the fables to actual gods, do anything rather than add to their divine character; for they do not perceive, that by the very defense they make for the gods, they confirm the things which are alleged concerning them. What have Europa, and the bull, and the swan, and Leda, to do with the earth and air, that the abominable intercourse of Zeus with them should be taken for the intercourse of the earth and air? But missing to discover the greatness of God, and not being able to rise on high with their reason (for they have no affinity for the heavenly place), they pine away among the forms of matter, and rooted to the earth, deify the changes of the elements: just as if any one should put the ship he sailed in the place of the steersman. But as the ship, although equipped with everything, is of no use if it has not a steersman, so neither are the elements, though arranged in perfect order, of any service apart from the providence of God. For the ship will not sail of itself; and the elements without their Framer will not move.

CHAPTER XXIII. —OPINIONS OF THALES AND PLATO.

You may say, however, since you excel all men in understanding, How comes it to pass, then, that some of the idols manifest power, if those to whom we erect the statues are not gods? For it is not likely that images destitute of life and motion can of themselves do anything without a mover. That in various places, cities, and nations, certain effects are brought about in the name of idols, we are far from denying. None the more, however, if some have received benefit, and others, on the contrary, suffered harm, shall we deem those to be gods who have produced the effects in either case. But I have made careful inquiry, both why it is that you think the idols to have this power, and who they are that, usurping their names, produce the effects. It is necessary for me, however, in attempting to show who they are that produce the effects ascribed to the idols, and that they are not gods, to have recourse to some witnesses from among the philosophers. First Thales, as those who have accurately examined his opinions report, divides [superior beings] into God, demons, and heroes.

God he recognizes as the Intelligence (νοῦς) of the world; by demons he understands beings possessed of soul (ψυχικαί); and by heroes the separated souls of men, the good being the good souls, and the bad the worthless. Plato again, while withholding his assent on other points, also divides [superior beings] into the uncreated God and those produced by the uncreated One for the adornment of heaven, the planets, and the fixed stars, and into demons; concerning which demons, while he does not think fit to speak himself, he thinks that those ought to be listened to who have spoken about them. "To speak concerning the other demons, and to know their origin, is beyond our powers; but we ought to believe those who have before spoken, the descendants of gods, as they say—and surely they must be well acquainted with their own ancestors: it is impossible, therefore, to disbelieve the sons of gods, even though they speak without probable or convincing proofs; but as they profess to tell of their own family affairs, we are bound, in pursuance of custom, to believe them. In this way, then, let us hold and speak as they do concerning the origin of the gods themselves. Of Gê and Ouranos were born Oceanus and Tethys; and of these Phorcus, Kronos, and Rhea, and the rest; and of Kronos and Rhea, Zeus, Hera, and all the others, who, we know, are all called their brothers; besides other descendants again of these." Did, then, he who had contemplated the eternal Intelligence and God who is apprehended by reason, and declared His attributes—His real existence, the simplicity of His nature, the good that flows forth from Him that is truth, and discoursed of primal power, and how "all things are about the King of all, and all things exist for His sake, and He is the cause of all;" and about two and three, that He is "the second moving about the seconds, and the third about the thirds;"—did this man think, that to learn the truth concerning those who are said to have been produced from sensible things, namely earth and heaven, was a task transcending his powers? It is not to be believed for a moment. But because he thought it impossible to believe that gods beget and are brought forth, since everything that begins to be is followed by an end, and (for this is much more difficult) to change the views of the multitude, who receive the fables without examination, on this account it was that he declared it to be beyond his powers to know and to speak concerning the origin of the other demons, since he was unable either to admit or teach that gods were begotten. And about that saying of his, "The great sovereign in heaven, Zeus, driving a winged car, advances first, ordering and managing all things, and there follow him a host of gods and demons," this does not refer to the Zeus who is said to have sprung from Kronos; for here the name is given to the Maker of the universe. This is shown by Plato himself: not being able to designate Him by another title that should be suitable, he availed himself of the popular name, not as peculiar to God, but for distinctness, because it is not possible to discourse of God to all men as fully as one might; and he adds at the same time the epithet "Great," so as to distinguish the heavenly from the earthly, the uncreated from the created, who is younger than heaven and earth, and younger than the Cretans, who stole him away, that he might not be killed by his father.

CHAPTER XXIV. —CONCERNING THE ANGELS AND GIANTS.

What need is there, in speaking to you who have searched into every department of knowledge, to mention the poets, or to examine opinions of another kind? Let it suffice to say thus much. If the poets and philosophers did not acknowledge that there is one God, and concerning these gods were not of opinion, some that they are demons, others that they are matter, and others that they once were men, —there might be some show of reason for our being harassed as we are, since we employ language which makes a distinction between God and matter, and the natures of the two. For, as we acknowledge a God, and a Son his Logos, and a Holy Spirit, united in essence,—the Father, the Son, the Spirit, because the Son is the Intelligence, Reason, Wisdom of the Father, and the Spirit an effluence, as light from fire; so also do we apprehend the existence of other powers, which exercise dominion about matter, and by means of it, and one in particular, which is hostile to God: not that anything is really opposed to God, like strife to friendship, according to Empedocles, and night to day, according to the appearing and disappearing of the stars (for even if anything *had* placed itself in opposition to God, it would have ceased to exist, its structure being destroyed by the power and might of God), but that to the good that is in God, which belongs of necessity to Him, and co-exists with Him, as color with body, without which it has no existence (not as being part of it, but as an attendant property co-existing with it, united and blended, just as it is natural for fire to be yellow and the ether dark blue),—to the good that is in God, I say, the spirit which is about matter, who was created by God, just as the other angels were created by Him, and entrusted with the control of matter and the forms of matter, is opposed. For this is the office of the angels, —to exercise providence for God over the things created and ordered by Him; so that God may have the universal and general providence of the whole, while the particular parts are provided for by the angels appointed over them. Just as with men, who have freedom of choice as to both virtue and vice (for you would not either honor the good or punish the bad, unless vice and virtue were in their own power; and some are diligent in the matters entrusted to them by you, and others faithless), so is it among the angels. Some, free agents, you will observe, such as they were created by God, continued in those things for which God had made and over which He had ordained them; but some outraged both the constitution of their nature and the government entrusted to them: namely, this ruler of matter and its various forms, and others of those who were placed about this first firmament (you know that we say nothing without witnesses, but state the things which have been declared by the prophets); these fell into impure love of virgins, and were subjugated by the flesh, and he became negligent and wicked in the management of the things entrusted to him. Of these lovers of virgins, therefore, were begotten those who are called giants. And if something has been said by the poets, too, about the giants, be not surprised at this: worldly wisdom and divine differ as much from each other as truth and plausibility: the one is of heaven and the other of earth; and indeed, according to the prince of matter, —

"We know we oft speak lies that look like truths."

CHAPTER XXV. —THE POETS AND PHILOSOPHERS HAVE DENIED A DIVINE PROVIDENCE.

These angels, then, who have fallen from heaven, and haunt the air and the earth, and are no longer able to rise to heavenly things, and the souls of the giants, which are the demons who wander about the world, perform actions similar, the one (that is, the demons) to the natures they have received, the other (that is, the angels) to the appetites they have indulged. But the prince of matter, as may be seen merely from what transpires, exercises a control and management contrary to the good that is in God: —

> "Ofttimes this anxious thought has crossed my mind,
> Whether 'tis chance or deity that rules
> The small affairs of men; and, spite of hope
> As well as justice, drives to exile some
> Stripped of all means of life, while others still
> Continue to enjoy prosperity."

Prosperity and adversity, contrary to hope and justice, made it impossible for Euripides to say to whom belongs the administration of earthly affairs, which is of such a kind that one might say of it: —

> "How then, while seeing these things, can we say
> There is a race of gods, or yield to laws?"

The same thing led Aristotle to say that the things below the heaven are not under the care of Providence, although the eternal providence of God concerns itself equally with us below, —

"The earth, let willingness move her or not,
Must herbs produce, and thus sustain my flocks,"—

and addresses itself to the deserving individually, according to truth and not according to opinion; and all other things, according to the general constitution of nature, are provided for by the law of reason. But because the demoniac movements and operations proceeding from the adverse spirit produce these disorderly sallies, and moreover move men, some in one way and some in another, as individuals and as nations, separately and in common, in accordance with the tendency of matter on the one hand, and of the affinity for divine things on the other, from within and from without,—some who are of no mean reputation have therefore thought that this universe is constituted without any definite order, and is driven hither and thither by an irrational chance. But they do not understand, that of those things which belong to the constitution of the whole world there is nothing out of order or neglected, but that each one of them has been produced by reason, and that, therefore, they do not transgress the order prescribed to them; and that man himself, too, so far as He that made him is concerned, is well ordered, both by his original nature, which has one common character for all, and by the constitution of his body, which does not transgress the law imposed upon it, and by the termination of his life, which remains equal and common to all alike; but that, according to the character peculiar to himself and the operation of the ruling prince and of the demons his followers, he is impelled and moved in this direction or in that, notwithstanding that all possess in common the same original constitution of mind.

CHAPTER XXVI. —THE DEMONS ALLURE MEN TO THE WORSHIP OF IMAGES.

They who draw men to idols, then, are the aforesaid demons, who are eager for the blood of the sacrifices, and lick them; but the gods that please the multitude, and whose names are given to the images, were men, as may be learned from their history. And that it is the demons who act under their names, is proved by the nature of their operations. For some castrate, as Rhea; others wound and slaughter, as Artemis; the Tauric goddess puts all strangers to death. I pass over those who lacerate with knives and scourges of bones and shall not attempt to describe all the kinds of demons; for it is not the part of a god to incite to things against nature.

"But when the demon plots against a man,
He first inflicts some hurt upon his mind."

But God, being perfectly good, is eternally doing good. That, moreover, those who exert the power are not the same as those to whom the statues are erected, very strong evidence is afforded by Troas and Parium. The one has statues of Neryllinus, a man of our own times; and Parium of Alexander and Proteus: both the sepulchre and the statue of Alexander are still in the forum. The other statues of Neryllinus, then, are a public ornament, if indeed a city can be adorned by such objects as these; but one of them is supposed to utter oracles and to heal the sick, and on this account the people of the Troad offer sacrifices to this statue, and overlay it with gold, and hang chaplets upon it. But of the statues of Alexander and Proteus (the latter, you are aware, threw himself into the fire near Olympia), that of Proteus is likewise said to utter oracles; and to that of Alexander—

"Wretched Paris, though in form so fair,
Thou slave of woman"—

sacrifices are offered and festivals are held at the public cost, as to a god who can hear. Is it, then, Neryllinus, and Proteus, and Alexander who exert these energies in connection with the statues, or is it the nature of the matter itself? But the matter is brass. And what can brass do of itself, which may be made again into a different form, as Amasis treated the footpan, as told by Herodotus? And Neryllinus, and Proteus, and Alexander, what good are they to the sick? For what the image is said now to effect, it effected when Neryllinus was alive and sick.

CHAPTER XXVII. —ARTIFICES OF THE DEMONS.

What then? In the first place, the irrational and fantastic movements of the soul about opinions produce a diversity of images (εἴδωλα) from time to time: some they derive from matter, and some they fashion and bring forth for themselves; and this happens to a soul especially when it partakes of the material spirit and becomes mingled with it, looking not at heavenly things and their Maker, but downwards to earthly things, wholly at the earth, as being now mere flesh and blood, and no longer pure spirit. These irrational and fantastic movements of the soul, then, give birth to empty visions in the mind, by which it becomes madly set on idols. When, too, a tender and susceptible soul, which has no knowledge or experience of sounder doctrines, and is unaccustomed to contemplate truth, and to consider thoughtfully the Father and Maker of all things, gets impressed with false opinions respecting itself, then the demons who hover about matter, greedy of sacrificial odors and the blood of victims, and ever ready to lead men into error, avail themselves of these delusive movements of the souls of the multitude; and, taking possession of their thoughts, cause to flow into the mind empty visions as if coming from the idols and the statues; and when, too, a soul of itself, as being immortal, moves comfortably to reason, either predicting the future or healing the present, the demons claim the glory for themselves.

CHAPTER XXVIII. —THE HEATHEN GODS WERE SIMPLY MEN.

But it is perhaps necessary, in accordance with what has already been adduced, to say a little about their names. Herodotus, then, and Alexander the son of Philip, in his letter to his mother (and each of them is said to have conversed with the priests at Heliopolis, and Memphis, and Thebes), affirm that they learnt from them that the gods had been men. Herodotus speaks thus: "Of such a nature were, they said, the beings represented by these images, they were very far indeed from being gods. However, in the times anterior to them it was otherwise; then Egypt had gods for its rulers, who dwelt upon the earth with men, one being always supreme above the rest. The last of these was Horus the son of Osiris, called by the Greeks Apollo. He deposed Typhon and ruled over Egypt as its last god-king. Osiris is named Dionysus (Bacchus) by the Greeks." "Almost all the names of the gods came into Greece from Egypt." Apollo was the son of Dionysus and Isis, as Herodotus likewise affirms: "According to the Egyptians, Apollo and Diana are the children of Bacchus and Isis; while Latona is their nurse and their preserver." These beings of heavenly origin they had for their first kings: partly from ignorance of the true worship of the Deity, partly from gratitude for their government, they esteemed them as gods together with their wives. "The male kine, if clean, and the male calves, are used for sacrifice by the Egyptians universally; but the females, they are not allowed to sacrifice, since they are sacred to Isis. The statue of this goddess has the form of a woman but with horns like a cow, resembling those of the Greek representations of Io." And who can be more deserving of credit in making these statements, than those who in family succession son from father, received not only the priesthood, but also the history? For it is not likely that the priests, who make it their business to commend the idols to men's reverence, would assert falsely that they were men. If Herodotus alone had said that the Egyptians spoke in their histories of the gods as of men, when he says, "What they told me concerning their religion it is not my intention to repeat, except only the names of their deities, things of very trifling importance," it would behoove us not to credit even Herodotus as being a fabulist. But as Alexander and Hermes surnamed Trismegistus, who shares with them in the attribute of eternity, and innumerable others, not to name them individually, [declare the same], no room is left even for doubt that they, being kings, were esteemed gods. That they were men, the most learned of the Egyptians also testify, who, while saying that ether, earth, sun, moon, are gods, regard the rest as mortal men, and the temples as their sepulchers. Apollodorus, too, asserts the same thing in his treatise concerning the gods. But Herodotus calls even their sufferings mysteries. "The ceremonies at the feast of Isis in the city of Busiris have been already spoken of. It is there that the whole multitude, both of men and women, many thousands in number, beat themselves at the close of the sacrifice in honor of a god whose name a religious scruple forbids me to mention." If they are gods, they are also immortal; but if people are beaten for them, and their sufferings are mysteries, they are men, as Herodotus himself says: "Here, too, in this same precinct of Minerva at Saïs, is the burial-place of one whom I think it not right to mention in such a connection. It stands behind the temple against the back wall, which it entirely covers. There are also some large stone obelisks in the enclosure, and there is a lake near them, adorned with an edging of stone. In form it is circular, and in size, as it seemed to me, about equal to the lake at Delos called the Hoop. On this lake it is that the Egyptians represent by night his sufferings whose name I refrain from mentioning, and this representation they call their mysteries." And not only is the sepulcher of Osiris shown, but also his embalming: "When a body is brought to them, they show the bearer various models of corpses made in wood and painted so as to resemble nature. The most perfect is said to be after the manner of him whom I do not think it religious to name in connection with such a matter."

CHAPTER XXIX. —*PROOF OF THE SAME FROM THE POETS.*

But among the Greeks, also, those who are eminent in poetry and history say the same thing. Thus of Heracles: —

"That lawless wretch, that man of brutal strength,
Deaf to Heaven's voice, the social rite transgressed."

Such being his nature, deservedly did he go mad, and deservedly did he light the funeral pile and burn himself to death. Of Asklepius, Hesiod says: —

"The mighty father both of gods and men
Was filled with wrath, and from Olympus' top
With flaming thunderbolt cast down and slew
Latona's well-lov'd son—such was his ire."

And Pindar: —

"But even wisdom is ensnared by gain.
The brilliant bribe of gold seen in the hand
Ev'n him perverted: therefore Kronos' son
With both hands quickly stopp'd his vital breath,
And by a bolt of fire ensured his doom."

Either, therefore, they were gods and did not hanker after gold—

"O gold, the fairest prize to mortal men,
Which neither mother equals in delight,
Nor children dear"—

for the Deity is in want of naught, and is superior to carnal desire, nor did they die; or, having been born men, they were wicked by reason of ignorance, and overcome by love of money. What more need I say, or refer to Castor, or Pollux, or Amphiaraus, who, having been born, so to speak, only the other day, men of men, are looked upon as gods, when they imagine even Ino after her madness and its consequent sufferings to have become a goddess?

"Sea-rovers will her name Leucothea."

And her son: —

"August Palæmon, sailors will invoke."

CHAPTER XXX. —REASONS WHY DIVINITY HAS BEEN ASCRIBED TO MEN.

For if detestable and god-hated men had the reputation of being gods, and the daughter of Derceto, Semiramis, a lascivious and blood-stained woman, was esteemed a Syria goddess; and if, on account of Derceto, the Syrians worship doves and Semiramis (for, a thing impossible, a woman was changed into a dove: the story is in Ctesias), what wonder if some should be called gods by their people on the ground of their rule and sovereignty (the Sibyl, of whom Plato also makes mention, says:—

"It was the generation then the tenth,
Of men endow'd with speech, since forth the flood
Had burst upon the men of former times,
And Kronos, Japetus, and Titan reigned,
Whom men, of Ouranos and Gaïa
Proclaimed the noblest sons, and named them so,
Because of men endowed with gift of speech
They were the first");

and others for their strength, as Heracles and Perseus; and others for their art, as Asclepius? Those, therefore, to whom either the subjects gave honor or the rulers themselves [assumed it], obtained the name, some from fear, others from revenge. Thus Antinous, through the benevolence of your ancestors towards their subjects, came to be regarded as a god. But those who came after adopted the worship without examination.

> "The Cretans always lie; for they, O king,
> Have built a tomb to thee who art not dead."

Though you believe, O Callimachus, in the nativity of Zeus, you do not believe in his sepulcher; and whilst you think to obscure the truth, you in fact proclaim him dead, even to those who are ignorant; and if you see the cave, you call to mind the childbirth of Rhea; but when you see the coffin, you throw a shadow over his death, not considering that the unbegotten
God alone is eternal. For either the tales told by the multitude and the poets about the gods are unworthy of credit, and the reverence shown them is superfluous (for those do not exist, the tales concerning whom are untrue); or if the births, the amours, the murders, the thefts, the castrations, the thunderbolts, are true, they no longer exist, having ceased to be since they were born, having previously had no being. And on what principle must we believe some things and disbelieve others, when the poets have written their stories in order to gain greater veneration for them? For surely those through whom they have got to be considered gods, and who have striven to represent their deeds as worthy of reverence, cannot have invented their sufferings. That, therefore, we are not atheists, acknowledging as we do God the Maker of this universe and His Logos, has been proved according to my ability, if not according to the importance of the subject.

CHAPTER XXXI. —CONFUTATION OF THE OTHER CHARGES BROUGHT AGAINST THE CHRISTIANS.

But they have further also made up stories against us of impious feasts and forbidden intercourse between the sexes, both that they may appear to themselves to have rational grounds of hatred, and because they think either by fear to lead us away from our way of life, or to render the rulers harsh and inexorable by the magnitude of the charges they bring. But they lose their labor with those who know that from of old it has been the custom, and not in our time only, for vice to make war on virtue. Thus Pythagoras, with three hundred others, was burnt to death; Heraclitus and Democritus were banished, the one from the city of the Ephesians, the other from Abdera, because he was charged with being mad; and the Athenians condemned Socrates to death. But as they were none the worse in respect of virtue because of the opinion of the multitude, so neither does the undiscriminating calumny of some persons cast any shade upon us about rectitude of life, for with God we stand in good repute. Nevertheless, I will meet these charges also, although I am well assured that by what has been already said I have cleared myself to you. For as you excel all men in intelligence, you know that those whose life is directed towards God as its rule, so that each one among us may be blameless and irreproachable before Him, will not entertain even the thought of the slightest sin. For if we believed that we should live only the present life, then we might be suspected of sinning, through being enslaved to flesh and blood, or overmastered by gain or carnal desire; but since we know that God is witness to what we think and what we say both by night and by day, and that He, being Himself light, sees all things in our heart, we are persuaded that when we are removed from the present life we shall live another life, better than the present one, and heavenly, not earthly (since we shall abide near God, and with God, free from all change or suffering in the soul, not as flesh, even though we shall have flesh, but as heavenly spirit), or, falling with the rest, a worse one and in fire; for God has not made us as sheep or beasts of burden, a mere by-work, and that we should perish and be annihilated. On these grounds it is not likely that we should wish to do evil or deliver ourselves over to the great Judge to be punished.

CHAPTER XXXII. —ELEVATED MORALITY OF THE CHRISTIANS.

It is, however, nothing wonderful that they should get up tales about us such as they tell of their own gods, of the incidents of whose lives they make mysteries. But it behooved them, if they meant to condemn shameless and promiscuous intercourse, to hate either Zeus, who begat children of his mother Rhea and his daughter Koré, and took his own sister to wife, or Orpheus, the inventor of these tales, which made Zeus more unholy and detestable than Thyestes himself; for the latter defiled his daughter in pursuance of an oracle, and when he wanted to obtain the kingdom and avenge himself. But we are so far from practicing promiscuous intercourse, that it is not lawful among us to indulge even a lustful look. "For," saith He, "he that looketh on a woman to lust after her, hath committed adultery already in his heart." Those, then, who are forbidden to look at anything more than that for which God formed the eyes, which were intended to be a light to us, and to whom a wanton look is adultery, the eyes being made for other purposes, and who are to be called to account for their very thoughts, how can any one doubt that such persons practice self-control? For our account lies not with human laws, which a bad man can evade (at the outset I proved to you, sovereign lords, that our doctrine is from the teaching of God), but we have a law which makes the measure of rectitude to consist in dealing with our neighbor as ourselves. On this account, too, according to age, we recognize some as sons and daughters, others we regard as brothers and sisters, and to the more advanced in life we give the honor due to fathers and mothers. On behalf of those, then, to whom we apply the names of brothers and sisters, and other designations of relationship, we exercise the greatest care that their bodies should remain undefiled and uncorrupted; for the Logos again says to us, "If any one kiss a second time because it has given him pleasure, [he sins];" adding, "Therefore the kiss, or rather the salutation, should be given with the greatest care, since, if there be mixed with it the least defilement of thought, it excludes us from eternal life."

CHAPTER XXXIII. —CHASTITY OF THE CHRISTIANS WITH RESPECT TO MARRIAGE.

Therefore, having the hope of eternal life, we despise the things of this life, even to the pleasures of the soul, each of us reckoning her his wife whom he has married according to the laws laid down by us, and that only for the purpose of having children. For as the husbandman throwing the seed into the ground awaits the harvest, not sowing more upon it, so to us the procreation of children is the measure of our indulgence in appetite. Nay, you would find many among us, both men and women, growing old unmarried, in hope of living in closer communion with God. But if the remaining in virginity and in the state of a eunuch brings nearer to God, while the indulgence of carnal thought and desire leads away from Him, in those cases in which we shun the thoughts, much more do we reject the deeds. For we bestow our attention, not on the study of words, but on the exhibition and teaching of actions, —that a person should either remain as he was born, or be content with one marriage; for a second marriage is only a specious adultery. "For whosoever puts away his wife," says He, "and marries another, commits adultery;" not permitting a man to send her away whose virginity he has brought to an end, nor to marry again. For he who deprives himself of his first wife, even though she be dead, is a cloaked adulterer, resisting the hand of God, because in the beginning God made one man and one woman, and dissolving the strictest union of flesh with flesh, formed for the intercourse of the race.

CHAPTER XXXIV. —THE VAST DIFFERENCE IN MORALS BETWEEN THE CHRISTIANS AND THEIR ACCUSERS.

But though such is our character (Oh! why should I speak of things unfit to be uttered?), the things said of us are an example of the proverb, "The harlot reproves the chaste." For those who have set up a market for fornication and established infamous resorts for the young for every kind of vile pleasure,—who do not abstain even from males, males with males committing shocking abominations, outraging all the noblest and comeliest bodies in all sorts of ways, so dishonoring the fair workmanship of God (for beauty on earth is not self-made, but sent hither by the hand and will of God),—these men, I say, revile us for the very things which they are conscious of themselves, and ascribe to their own gods, boasting of them as noble deeds, and worthy of the gods. These adulterers and pæderasts defame the eunuchs and the once-married (while they themselves live like fishes; for these gulp down whatever falls in their way, and the stronger chases the weaker: and, in fact, this is to feed upon human flesh, to do violence in contravention of the very laws which you and your ancestors, with due care for all that is fair and right, have enacted), so that not even the governors of the provinces sent by you suffice for the hearing of the complaints against those, to whom it even is not lawful, when they are struck, not to offer themselves for more blows, nor when defamed not to bless: for it is not enough to be just (and justice is to return like for like), but it is incumbent on us to be good and patient of evil.

CHAPTER XXXV. —THE CHRISTIANS CONDEMN AND DETEST ALL CRUELTY.

What man of sound mind, therefore, will affirm, while such is our character, that we are murderers? For we cannot eat human flesh till we have killed some one. The former charge, therefore, being false, if any one should ask them regarding the second, whether they have seen what they assert, not one of them would be so barefaced as to say that he had. And yet we have slaves, some more and some fewer, by whom we could not help being seen; but even of these, not one has been found to invent even such things against us. For when they know that we cannot endure even to see a man put to death, though justly; who of them can accuse us of murder or cannibalism? Who does not reckon among the things of greatest interest the contests of gladiators and wild beasts, especially those which are given by you? But we, deeming that to see a man put to death is much the same as killing him, have abjured such spectacles. How, then, when we do not even look on, lest we should contract guilt and pollution, can we put people to death? And when we say that those women who use drugs to bring on abortion commit murder, and will have to give an account to God for the abortion, on what principle should we commit murder? For it does not belong to the same person to regard the very foetus in the womb as a created being, and therefore an object of God's care, and when it has passed into life, to kill it; and not to expose an infant, because those who expose them are chargeable with child-murder, and on the other hand, when it has been reared to destroy it. But we are in all things always alike and the same, submitting ourselves to reason, and not ruling over it.

CHAPTER XXXVI. —BEARING OF THE DOCTRINE OF THE RESURRECTION ON THE PRACTICES OF THE CHRISTIANS.

Who, then, that believes in a resurrection, would make himself into a tomb for bodies that will rise again? For it is not the part of the same persons to believe that our bodies will rise again, and to eat them as if they would not; and to think that the earth will give back the bodies held by it, but that those which a man has entombed in himself will not be demanded back. On the contrary, it is reasonable to suppose, that those who think they shall have no account to give of the present life, ill or well spent, and that there is no resurrection, but calculate on the soul perishing with the body, and being as it were quenched in it, will refrain from no deed of daring; but as for those who are persuaded that nothing will escape the scrutiny of God, but that even the body which has ministered to the irrational impulses of the soul, and to its desires, will be punished along with it, it is not likely that they will commit even the smallest sin. But if to any one it appears sheer nonsense that the body which has mouldered away, and been dissolved, and reduced to nothing, should be reconstructed, we certainly cannot with any reason be accused of wickedness with reference to those that believe not, but only of folly; for with the opinions by which we deceive ourselves we injure no one else. But that it is not our belief alone that bodies will rise again, but that many philosophers also hold the same view, it is out of place to show just now, lest we should be thought to introduce topics irrelevant to the matter in hand, either by speaking of the intelligible and the sensible, and the nature of these respectively, or by contending that the incorporeal is older than the corporeal, and that the intelligible precedes the sensible, although we become acquainted with the latter earliest, since the corporeal is formed from the incorporeal, by the combination with it of the intelligible, and that the sensible is formed from the intelligible; for nothing hinders, according to Pythagoras and Plato, that when the dissolution of bodies takes place, they should, from the very same elements of which they were constructed at first, be constructed again. But let us defer the discourse concerning the resurrection.

CHAPTER XXXVII. —ENTREATY TO BE FAIRLY JUDGED.

And now do you, who are entirely in everything, by nature and by education, upright, and moderate, and benevolent, and worthy of your rule, now that I have disposed of the several accusations, and proved that we are pious, and gentle, and temperate in spirit, bend your royal head in approval. For who are more deserving to obtain the things they ask, than those who, like us, pray for your government, that you may, as is most equitable, receive the kingdom, son from father, and that your empire may receive increase and addition, all men becoming subject to your sway? And this is also for our advantage, that we may lead a peaceable and quiet life, and may ourselves readily perform all that is commanded us.

THE TREATISE OF ATHENAGORAS

The Athenian, Philosopher and Christian, on the Resurrection of the Dead.

CHAPTER I.—DEFENCE OF THE TRUTH SHOULD PRECEDE DISCUSSIONS REGARDING IT.

By the side of every opinion and doctrine which agrees with the truth of things, there springs up some falsehood; and it does so, not because it takes its rise naturally from some fundamental principle, or from some cause peculiar to the matter in hand, but because it is invented on purpose by men who set a value on the spurious seed, for its tendency to corrupt the truth. This is apparent, in the first place, from those who in former times addicted themselves to such inquiries, and their want of agreement with their predecessors and contemporaries, and then, not least, from the very confusion which marks the discussions that are now going on. For such men have left no truth free from their calumnious attacks—not the being of God, not His knowledge, not His operations, not those books which follow by a regular and strict sequence from these, and delineate for us the doctrines of piety. On the contrary, some of them utterly, and once for all, give up in despair the truth concerning these things, and some distort it to suit their own views, and some of set purpose doubt even of things which are palpably evident. Hence I think that those who bestow attention on such subjects should adopt two lines of argument, one in defense of the truth, another concerning the truth: that in defense of the truth, for disbelievers and doubters; that concerning the truth, for such as are candid and receive the truth with readiness. Accordingly, it behooves those who wish to investigate these matters, to keep in view that which the necessity of the case in each instance requires, and to regulate their discussion by this; to accommodate the order of their treatment of these subjects to what is suitable to the occasion, and not for the sake of appearing always to preserve the same method, to disregard fitness and the place which properly belongs to each topic. For, so far as proof and the natural order are concerned, dissertations concerning the truth always take precedence of those in defense of it; but, for the purpose of greater utility, the order must be reversed, and arguments in defense of it precede those concerning it. For the farmer could not properly cast the seed into the ground, unless he first extirpated the wild wood, and whatever would be hurtful to the good seed; nor the physician introduce any wholesome medicines into the body that needed his care, if he did not previously remove the disease within, or stay that which was approaching. Neither surely can he who wishes to teach the truth persuade any one by speaking about it, so long as there is a false opinion lurking in the mind of his hearers, and barring the entrance of his arguments. And, therefore, from regard to greater utility, I myself sometimes place arguments in defense of the truth before those concerning the truth; and on the present occasion it appears to me, looking at the requirements of the case, not without advantage to follow the same method in treating of the resurrection. For in regard to this subject also we find some utterly disbelieving, and some others doubting, and even among those who have accepted the first principles some who are as much at a loss what to believe as those who doubt; the most unaccountable thing of all being, that they are in this state of mind without having any ground whatsoever in the matters themselves for their disbelief, or finding it possible to assign any reasonable cause why they disbelieve or experience any perplexity.

CHAPTER II. —A RESURRECTION IS NOT IMPOSSIBLE.

Let us, then, consider the subject in the way I have indicated. If all disbelief does not arise from levity and inconsideration, but if it springs up in some minds on strong grounds and accompanied by the certainty which belongs to truth [well and good]; for it then maintains the appearance of being just, when the thing itself to which their disbelief relates appears to them unworthy of belief; but to disbelieve things which are not deserving of disbelief, is the act of men who do not employ a sound judgment about the truth. It behooves, therefore, those who disbelieve or doubt concerning the resurrection, to form their opinion on the subject, not from any view they have hastily adopted, and from what is acceptable to profligate men, but either to assign the origin of men to no cause (a notion which is very easily refuted), or, ascribing the cause of all things to God, to keep steadily in view the principle involved in this article of belief, and from this to demonstrate that the resurrection is utterly unworthy of credit. This they will succeed in, if they are able to show that it is either impossible for God, or contrary to His will, to unite and gather together again bodies that are dead, or even entirely dissolved into their elements, so as to constitute the same persons. If they cannot do this, let them cease from this godless disbelief, and from this blasphemy against sacred things: for, that they do not speak the truth when they say that it is impossible, or not in accordance with the divine will, will clearly appear from what I am about to say. A thing is in strictness of language considered impossible to a person, when it is of such a kind that he either does not know what is to be done or has not sufficient power for the proper doing of the thing known. For he who is ignorant of anything that requires to be done, is utterly unable either to attempt or to do what he is ignorant of; and he, too, who knows ever so well what has to be done, and by what means, and how, but either has no power at all to do the thing known, or not power sufficient, will not even make the attempt, if he be wise and consider his powers; and if he did attempt it without due consideration, he would not accomplish his purpose. But it is not possible for God to be ignorant, either of the nature of the bodies that are to be raised, as regards both the members entire and the particles of which they consist, or whither each of the dissolved particles passes, and what part of the elements has received that which is dissolved and has passed into that with which it has affinity, although to men it may appear quite impossible that what has again combined according to its nature with the universe should be separable from it again. For He from whom, antecedently to the peculiar formation of each, was not concealed either the nature of the elements of which the bodies of men were to consist, or the parts of these from which He was about to take what seemed to Him suitable for the formation of the human body, will manifestly, after the dissolution of the whole, not be ignorant whither each of the particles has passed which He took for the construction of each. For, viewed relatively to the order of things now obtaining among us, and the judgment we form concerning other matters, it is a greater thing to know beforehand that which has not yet come to pass; but, viewed relatively to the majesty and wisdom of God, both are according to nature, and it is equally easy to know beforehand things that have not yet come into existence, and to know things which have been dissolved.

CHAPTER III. —HE WHO COULD CREATE, CAN ALSO RAISE UP THE DEAD.

Moreover also, that His power is sufficient for the raising of dead bodies, is shown by the creation of these same bodies. For if, when they did not exist, He made at their first formation the bodies of men, and their original elements, He will, when they are dissolved, in whatever manner that may take place, raise them again with equal ease: for this, too, is equally possible to Him. And it is no damage to the argument, if some suppose the first beginnings to be from matter, or the bodies of men at least to be derived from the elements as the first materials, or from seed. For that power which could give shape to what is regarded by them as shapeless matter, and adorn it, when destitute of form and order, with many and diverse forms, and gather into one the several portions of the elements, and divide the seed which was one and simple into many, and organize that which was unorganized, and give life to that which had no life,—that same power can reunite what is dissolved, and raise up what is prostrate, and restore the dead to life again, and put the corruptible into a state of incorruption. And to the same Being it will belong, and to the same power and skill, to separate that which has been broken up and distributed among a multitude of animals of all kinds which are wont to have recourse to such bodies, and glut their appetite upon them,—to separate this, I say, and unite it again with the proper members and parts of members, whether it has passed into some one of those animals, or into many, or thence into others, or, after being dissolved along with these, has been carried back again to the original elements, resolved into these according to a natural law—a matter this which seems to have exceedingly confounded some, even of those admired for wisdom, who, I cannot tell why, think those doubts worthy of serious attention which are brought forward by the many.

CHAPTER IV. —OBJECTION FROM THE FACT THAT SOME HUMAN BODIES HAVE BECOME PART OF OTHERS.

These persons, to wit, say that many bodies of those who have come to an unhappy death in shipwrecks and rivers have become food for fishes, and many of those who perish in war, or who from some other sad cause or state of things are deprived of burial, lie exposed to become the food of any animals which may chance to light upon them. Since, then, bodies are thus consumed, and the members and parts composing them are broken up and distributed among a great multitude of animals, and by means of nutrition become incorporated with the bodies of those that are nourished by them, —in the first place, they say, their separation from these is impossible; and besides this, in the second place, they adduce another circumstance more difficult still. When animals of the kind suitable for human food, which have fed on the bodies of men, pass through their stomach, and become incorporated with the bodies of those who have partaken of them, it is an absolute necessity, they say, that the parts of the bodies of men which have served as nourishment to the animals which have partaken of them should pass into other bodies of men, since the animals which meanwhile have been nourished by them convey the nutriment derived from those by whom they were nourished into those men of whom they become the nutriment. Then to this they tragically add the devouring of offspring perpetrated by people in famine and madness, and the children eaten by their own parents through the contrivance of enemies, and the celebrated Median feast, and the tragic banquet of Thyestes; and they add, moreover, other such like unheard-of occurrences which have taken place among Greeks and barbarians: and from these things they establish, as they suppose, the impossibility of the resurrection, on the ground that the same parts cannot rise again with one set of bodies, and with another as well; for that either the bodies of the former possessors cannot be reconstituted, the parts which composed them having passed into others, or that, these having been restored to the former, the bodies of the last possessors will come short.

CHAPTER V.—REFERENCE TO THE PROCESSES OF DIGESTION AND NUTRITION.

But it appears to me that such persons, in the first place, are ignorant of the power and skill of Him that fashioned and regulates this universe, who has adapted to the nature and kind of each animal the nourishment suitable and correspondent to it, and has neither ordained that everything in nature shall enter into union and combination with every kind of body, nor is at any loss to separate what has been so united, but grants to the nature of each several created being or thing to do or to suffer what is naturally suited to it, and sometimes also hinders and allows or forbids whatever He wishes, and for the purpose He wishes; and, moreover, that they have not considered the power and nature of each of the creatures that nourish or are nourished. Otherwise they would have known that not everything which is taken for food under the pressure of outward necessity turns out to be suitable nourishment for the animal, but that some things no sooner come into contact with the plicatures of the stomach than they are wont to be corrupted, and are vomited or voided, or disposed of in some other way, so that not even for a little time do they undergo the first and natural digestion, much less become incorporated with that which is to be nourished; as also, that not even everything which has been digested in the stomach and received the first change actually arrives at the parts to be nourished, since some of it loses its nutritive power even in the stomach, and some during the second change, and the digestion that takes place in the liver is separated and passes into something else which is destitute of the power to nourish; nay, that the change which takes place in the liver does not all issue in nourishment to men, but the matter changed is separated as refuse according to its natural purpose; and that the nourishment which is left in the members and parts themselves that have to be nourished sometimes changes to something else, according as that predominates which is present in greater or less abundance, and is apt to corrupt or to turn into itself that which comes near it.

CHAPTER VI. —EVERYTHING THAT IS USELESS OR HURTFUL IS REJECTED.

Since, therefore, great difference of nature obtains in all animals, and the very nourishment which is accordant with nature is varied to suit each kind of animal, and the body which is nourished; and as in the nourishment of every animal there is a threefold cleansing and separation, it follows that whatever is alien from the nourishment of the animal must be wholly destroyed and carried off to its natural place, or change into something else, since it cannot coalesce with it; that the power of the nourishing body must be suitable to the nature of the animal to be nourished, and accordant with its powers; and that this, when it has passed through the strainers appointed for the purpose, and been thoroughly purified by the natural means of purification, must become a most genuine addition to the substance,—the only thing, in fact, which any one calling things by their right names would call nourishment at all; because it rejects everything that is foreign and hurtful to the constitution of the animal nourished and that mass of superfluous food introduced merely for filling the stomach and gratifying the appetite. This nourishment, no one can doubt, becomes incorporated with the body that is nourished, interwoven and blended with all the members and parts of members; but that which is different and contrary to nature is speedily corrupted if brought into contact with a stronger power, but easily destroys that which is overcome by it, and is converted into hurtful humors and poisonous qualities, because producing nothing akin or friendly to the body which is to be nourished. And it is a very clear proof of this, that in many of the animals nourished, pain, or disease, or death follows from these things, if, owing to a too keen appetite, they take in mingled with their food something poisonous and contrary to nature; which, of course, would tend to the utter destruction of the body to be nourished, since that which is nourished is nourished by substances akin to it and which accord with its nature, but is destroyed by those of a contrary kind. If, therefore, according to the different nature of animals, different kinds of food have been provided suitable to their nature, and none of that which the animal may have taken, not even an accidental part of it, admits of being blended with the body which is nourished, but only that part which has been purified by an entire digestion, and undergone a complete change for union with a particular body, and adapted to the parts which are to receive nourishment,—it is very plain that none of the things contrary to nature can be united with those bodies for which it is not a suitable and correspondent nourishment, but either passes off by the bowels before it produces some other humor, crude and corrupted; or, if it continue for a longer time, produces suffering or disease hard to cure, destroying at the same time the natural nourishment, or even the flesh itself which needs nourishment. But even though it be expelled at length, overcome by certain medicines, or by better food, or by the natural forces, it is not got rid of without doing much harm, since it bears no peaceful aspect towards what is natural, because it cannot coalesce with nature.

CHAPTER VII. —THE RESURRECTION-BODY DIFFERENT FROM THE PRESENT.

Nay, suppose we were to grant that the nourishment coming from these things (let it be so called, as more accordant with the common way of speaking), although against nature, is yet separated and changed into some one of the moist or dry, or warm or cold, matters which the body contains, our opponents would gain nothing by the concession: for the bodies that rise again are reconstituted from the parts which properly belong to them, whereas no one of the things mentioned is such a part, nor has it the form or place of a part; nay, it does not remain always with the parts of the body which are nourished, or rise again with the parts that rise, since no longer does blood, or phlegm, or bile, or breath, contribute anything to the life. Neither, again, will the bodies nourished then require the things they once required, seeing that, along with the want and corruption of the bodies nourished, the need also of those things by which they were nourished is taken away. To this must be added, that if we were to suppose the change arising from such nourishment to reach as far as flesh, in that case too there would be no necessity that the flesh recently changed by food of that kind, if it became united to the body of some other man, should again as a part contribute to the formation of that body, since neither the flesh which takes it up always retains what it takes, nor does the flesh so incorporated abide and remain with that to which it was added, but is subject to a great variety of changes,—at one time being dispersed by toil or care, at another time being wasted by grief or trouble or disease, and by the distempers arising from being heated or chilled, the humors which are changed with the flesh and fat not receiving the nourishment so as to remain what they are. But while such are the changes to which the flesh is subject, we should find that flesh, nourished by food unsuited to it, suffers them in a much greater degree; now swelling out and growing fat by what it has received, and then again rejecting it in some way or other, and decreasing in bulk, from one or more of the causes already mentioned; and that that alone remains in the parts which is adapted to bind together, or cover, or warm the flesh that has been chosen by nature, and adheres to those parts by which it sustains the life which is according to nature, and fulfils the labors of that life. So that whether the investigation in which we have just been engaged be fairly judged of, or the objections urged against our position be conceded, in neither case can it be shown that what is said by our opponents is true, nor can the bodies of men ever combine with those of the same nature, whether at any time, through ignorance and being cheated of their perception by some one else, men have partaken of such a body, or of their own accord, impelled by want or madness, they have defiled themselves with the body of one of like form; for we are very well aware that some brutes have human forms, or have a nature compounded of men and brutes, such as the more daring of the poets are accustomed to represent.

CHAPTER VIII. —HUMAN FLESH NOT THE PROPER OR NATURAL FOOD OF MEN.

But what need is there to speak of bodies not allotted to be the food of any animal, and destined only for a burial in the earth in honor of nature, since the Maker of the world has not alloted any animal whatsoever as food to those of the same kind, although some others of a different kind serve for food according to nature? If, indeed, they are able to show that the flesh of men was alloted to men for food, there will be nothing to hinder its being according to nature that they should eat one another, just like anything else that is allowed by nature, and nothing to prohibit those who dare to say such things from regaling themselves with the bodies of their dearest friends as delicacies, as being especially suited to them, and to entertain their living friends with the same fare. But if it be unlawful even to speak of this, and if for men to partake of the flesh of men is a thing most hateful and abominable, and more detestable than any other unlawful and unnatural food or act; and if what is against nature can never pass into nourishment for the limbs and parts requiring it, and what does not pass into nourishment can never become united with that which it is not adapted to nourish,—then can the bodies of men never combine with bodies like themselves, to which this nourishment would be against nature, even though it were to pass many times through their stomach, owing to some most bitter mischance; but, removed from the influence of the nourishing power, and scattered to those parts of the universe again from which they obtained their first origin, they are united with these for as long a period of time as may be the lot of each; and, separated thence again by the skill and power of Him who has fixed the nature of every animal, and furnished it with its peculiar powers, they are united suitably, each to each, whether they have been burnt up by fire, or rotted by water, or consumed by wild beasts, or by any other animals, or separated from the entire body and dissolved before the other parts; and, being again united with one another, they occupy the same place for the exact construction and formation of the same body, and for the resurrection and life of that which was dead, or even entirely dissolved. To expatiate further, however, on these topics, is not suitable; for all men are agreed in their decision respecting them, —those at least who are not half brutes.

CHAPTER IX. —ABSURDITY OF ARGUING FROM MAN'S IMPOTENCY.

As there are many things of more importance to the inquiry before us, I beg to be excused from replying for the present to those who take refuge in the works of men, and even the constructors of them, who are unable to make anew such of their works as are broken in pieces, or worn out by time, or otherwise destroyed, and then from the analogy of potters and carpenters attempt to show that God neither can will, nor if He willed would be able, to raise again a body that is dead, or has been dissolved,—not considering that by such reasoning they offer the grossest insult to God, putting, as they do, on the same level the capabilities of things which are altogether different, or rather the natures of those who use them, and comparing the works of art with those of nature. To bestow any serious attention on such arguments would be not undeserving of censure, for it is really foolish to reply to superficial and trifling objections. It is surely far more probable, yea, most absolutely true, to say that what is impossible with men is possible with God. And if by this statement of itself as probable, and by the whole investigation in which we have just been engaged reason shows it to be possible, it is quite clear that it is not impossible. No, nor is it such a thing as God could not will.

CHAPTER X.—IT CANNOT BE SHOWN THAT GOD DOES NOT WILL A RESURRECTION.

For that which is not accordant with His will is so either as being unjust or as unworthy of Him. And again, the injustice regards either him who is to rise again, or some other than he. But it is evident that no one of the beings exterior to him, and that are reckoned among the things that have existence, is injured. Spiritual natures (νοηταὶ φύσεις) cannot be injured by the resurrection of men, for the resurrection of men is no hindrance to their existing, nor is any loss or violence inflicted on them by it; nor, again, would the nature of irrational or inanimate beings sustain wrong, for they will have no existence after the resurrection, and no wrong can be done to that which is not. But even if any one should suppose them to exist for ever, they would not suffer wrong by the renewal of human bodies: for if now, in being subservient to the nature of men and their necessities while they require them, and subjected to the yoke and every kind of drudgery, they suffer no wrong, much more, when men have become immortal and free from want, and no longer need their service, and when they are themselves liberated from bondage, will they suffer no wrong. For if they had the gift of speech, they would not bring against the Creator the charge of making them, contrary to justice, inferior to men because they did not share in the same resurrection. For to creatures whose nature is not alike the Just Being does not assign a like end. And, besides, with creatures that have no notion of justice there can be no complaint of injustice. Nor can it be said either that there is any injustice done about the man to be raised, for he consists of soul and body, and he suffers no wrong as to either soul or body. No person in his senses will affirm that his soul suffers wrong, because, in speaking so, he would at the same time be unawares reflecting on the present life also; for if now, while dwelling in a body subject to corruption and suffering, it has had no wrong done to it, much less will it suffer wrong when living in conjunction with a body which is free from corruption and suffering. The body, again, suffers no wrong; for if no wrong is done to it now while united a corruptible thing with an incorruptible, manifestly will it not be wronged when united an incorruptible with an incorruptible. No; nor can any one say that it is a work unworthy of God to raise up and bring together again a body which has been dissolved: for if the worse was not unworthy of Him, namely, to make the body which is subject to corruption and suffering, much more is the better not unworthy, to make one not liable to corruption or suffering.

CHAPTER XI.—RECAPITULATION.

If, then, by means of that which is by nature first and that which follows from it, each of the points investigated has been proved, it is very evident that the resurrection of dissolved bodies is a work which the Creator can perform, and can will, and such as is worthy of Him: for by these considerations the falsehood of the contrary opinion has been shown, and the absurdity of the position taken by disbelievers. For why should I speak of their correspondence each with each, and of their connection with one another? If indeed we ought to use the word connection, as though they were separated by some difference of nature; and not rather say, that what God can do He can also will, and that what God can will it is perfectly possible for Him to do, and that it is accordant with the dignity of Him who wills it. That to discourse concerning the truth is one thing, and to discourse in defense of it is another, has been sufficiently explained in the remarks already made, as also in what respects they differ from each other, and when and in dealing with whom they are severally useful; but perhaps there is no reason why, with a view to the general certainty, and because of the connection of what has been said with what remains, we should not make a fresh beginning from these same points and those which are allied to them. To the one kind of argument it naturally pertains to hold the foremost place, to the other to attend upon the first, and clear the way, and to remove whatever is obstructive or hostile. The discourse concerning the truth, as being necessary to all men for certainty and safety, holds the first place, whether in nature, or order, or usefulness: in nature, as furnishing the knowledge of the subject; in order, as being in those things and along with those things which it informs us of; in usefulness, as being a guarantee of certainty and safety to those who become acquainted with it. The discourse in defense of the truth is inferior in nature and force, for the refutation of falsehood is less important than the establishment of truth; and second in order, for it employs its strength against those who hold false opinions, and false opinions are an aftergrowth from another sowing and from degeneration. But, notwithstanding all this, it is often placed first, and sometimes is found more useful, because it removes and clears away beforehand the disbelief which disquiets some minds, and the doubt or false opinion of such as have but recently come over. And yet each of them is referrible to the same end, for the refutation of falsehood and the establishment of truth both have piety for their object: not, indeed, that they are absolutely one and the same, but the one is necessary, as I have said, to all who believe, and to those who are concerned about the truth and their own salvation; but the other proves to be more useful on some occasions, and to some persons, and in dealing with some. Thus much by way of recapitulation, to recall what has been already said. We must now pass on to what we proposed, and show the truth of the doctrine concerning the resurrection, both from the cause itself, according to which, and on account of which, the first man and his posterity were created, although they were not brought into existence in the same manner, and from the common nature of all men as men; and further, from the judgment of their Maker upon them according to the time each has lived, and according to the rules by which each has regulated his behavior,—a judgment which no one can doubt will be just.

CHAPTER XII. —ARGUMENT FOR THE RESURRECTION /ROM THE PURPOSE CONTEMPLATED IN MAN'S CREATION.

The argument from the cause will appear, if we consider whether man was made at random and in vain, or for some purpose; and if for some purpose, whether simply that he might live and continue in the natural condition in which he was created, or for the use of another; and if with a view to use, whether for that of the Creator Himself, or of some one of the beings who belong to Him, and are by Him deemed worthy of greater care. Now, if we consider this in the most general way, we find that a person of sound mind, and who is moved by a rational judgment to do anything, does nothing in vain which he does intentionally, but either for his own use, or for the use of some other person for whom he cares, or for the sake of the work itself, being moved by some natural inclination and affection towards its production. For instance (to make use of an illustration, that our meaning may be clear), a man makes a house for his own use, but for cattle and camels and other animals of which he has need he makes the shelter suitable for each of them; not for his own use, if we regard the appearance only, though for that, if we look at the end he has in view, but as regards the immediate object, from concern for those for whom he cares. He has children, too, not for his own use, nor for the sake of anything else belonging to him, but that those who spring from him may exist and continue as long as possible, thus by the succession of children and grandchildren comforting himself respecting the close of his own life, and hoping in this way to immortalize the mortal. Such is the procedure of men. But God can neither have made man in vain, for He is wise, and no work of wisdom is in vain; nor for His own use, for He is in want of nothing. But to a Being absolutely in need of nothing, no one of His works can contribute anything to His own use. Neither, again, did He make man for the sake of any of the other works which He has made. For nothing that is endowed with reason and judgment has been created, or is created, for the use of another, whether greater or less than itself, but for the sake of the life and continuance of the being itself so created. For reason cannot discover any use which might be deemed a cause for the creation of men, since immortals are free from want, and in need of no help from men in order to their existence; and irrational beings are by nature in a state of subjection, and perform those services for men for which each of them was intended, but are not intended in their turn to make use of men: for it neither was nor is right to lower that which rules and takes the lead to the use of the inferior, or to subject the rational to the irrational, which is not suited to rule. Therefore, if man has been created neither without cause and in vain (for none of God's works is in vain, so far at least as the purpose of their Maker is concerned), nor for the use of the Maker Himself, or of any of the works which have proceeded from Him, it is quite clear that although, according to the first and more general view of the subject, God made man for Himself, and in pursuance of the goodness and wisdom which are conspicuous throughout the creation, yet, according to the view which more nearly touches the beings created, He made him for the sake of the life of those created, which is not kindled for a little while and then extinguished. For to creeping things, I suppose, and birds, and fishes, or, to speak more generally, all irrational creatures, God has assigned such a life as that; but to those who bear upon them the image of the Creator Himself, and are endowed with understanding, and blessed with a rational judgment, the Creator has assigned perpetual duration, in order that, recognizing their own Maker, and His power and skill, and obeying law and justice, they may pass their whole existence free from suffering, in the possession of those qualities with which they have bravely borne their preceding life, although they lived in corruptible and earthly bodies. For whatever has been created for the sake of something else, when that has ceased to be for the sake of which it was created, will itself also fitly cease to be, and will not continue to exist in vain, since, among the works of God, that which is useless can have no place; but that which was created for the very purpose of existing and living a life naturally suited to it, since the cause itself is bound up with its nature, and is recognized only in connection with existence itself, can never admit of any cause which shall utterly annihilate its existence. But since this cause is seen to lie in perpetual existence, the being so created must be preserved for ever, doing and experiencing what is suitable to its nature, each of the two parts of which it consists contributing what belongs to it, so that the soul may exist and remain without change in the nature in which it was made, and discharge its appropriate functions (such as presiding over the impulses of the body, and judging of and measuring that which occurs from time to time by the proper standards and measures), and the body be moved according to its nature towards its appropriate objects, and undergo the changes allotted to it, and, among the rest (relating to age, or appearance, or size), the resurrection. For the resurrection is a species of change, and the last of all, and a change for the better of what still remains in existence at that time.

CHAPTER XIII. —CONTINUATION OF THE ARGUMENT.

Confident of these things, no less than of those which have already come to pass, and reflecting on our own nature, we are content with a life associated with neediness and corruption, as suited to our present state of existence, and we steadfastly hope for a continuance of being in immortality; and this we do not take without foundation from the inventions of men, feeding ourselves on false hopes, but our belief rests on a most infallible guarantee—the purpose of Him who fashioned us, according to which He made man of an immortal soul and a body, and furnished him with understanding and an innate law for the preservation and safeguard of the things given by Him as suitable to an intelligent existence and a rational life: for we know well that He would not have fashioned such a being, and furnished him with everything belonging to perpetuity, had He not intended that what was so created should continue in perpetuity. If, therefore, the Maker of this universe made man with a view to his partaking of an intelligent life, and that, having become a spectator of His grandeur, and of the wisdom which is manifest in all things, he might continue always in the contemplation of these; then, according to the purpose of his Author, and the nature which he has received, the cause of his creation is a pledge of his continuance for ever, and this continuance is a pledge of the resurrection, without which man could not continue. So that, from what has been said, it is quite clear that the resurrection is plainly proved by the cause of man's creation, and the purpose of Him who made him. Such being the nature of the cause for which man has been brought into this world, the next thing will be to consider that which immediately follows, naturally or in the order proposed; and in our investigation the cause of their creation is followed by the nature of the men so created, and the nature of those created by the just judgment of their Maker upon them, and all these by the end of their existence. Having investigated therefore the point placed first in order, we must now go on to consider the nature of men.

CHAPTER XIV. —THE RESURRECTION DOES NOT REST SOLELY ON THE FACT OF A FUTURE JUDGMENT.

The proof of the several doctrines of which the truth consists, or of any matter whatsoever proposed for examination, if it is to produce an unwavering confidence in what is said, must begin, not from anything without, nor from what certain persons think or have thought, but from the common and natural notion of the matter, or from the connection of secondary truths with primary ones. For the question relates either to primary beliefs, and then all that is necessary is reminiscence, so as to stir up the natural notion; or to things which naturally follow from the first and to their natural sequence. And in these things we must observe order, showing what strictly follows from the first truths, or from those which are placed first, so as neither to be unmindful of the truth, or of our certainty respecting it, nor to confound the things arranged by nature and distinguished from each other, or break up the natural order. Hence I think it behooves those who desire to handle the subject with fairness, and who wish to form an intelligent judgment whether there is a resurrection or not, first to consider attentively the force of the arguments contributing to the proof of this, and what place each of them holds—which is first, which second, which third, and which last. And in the arrangement of these they should place first the cause of the creation of men,—namely, the purpose of the Creator in making man; and then connect with this, as is suitable, the nature of the men so created; not as being second in order, but because we are unable to pass our judgment on both at the same time, although they have the closest natural connection with each other, and are of equal force in reference to the subject before us. But while from these proofs as the primary ones, and as being derived from the work of creation, the resurrection is clearly demonstrated, none the less can we gain conviction respecting it from the arguments taken from providence, —I mean from the reward or punishment due to each man in accordance with just judgment, and from the end of human existence. For many, in discussing the subject of the resurrection, have rested the whole cause on the third argument alone, deeming that the cause of the resurrection is the judgment. But the fallacy of this is very clearly shown, from the fact that, although all human beings who die rise again, yet not all who rise again are to be judged: for if only a just judgment were the cause of the resurrection, it would of course follow that those who had done neither evil nor good—namely, very young children—would not rise again; but seeing that all are to rise again, those who have died in infancy as well as others, they too justify our conclusion that the resurrection takes place not for the sake of the judgment as the primary reason, but in consequence of the purpose of God in forming men, and the nature of the beings so formed.

CHAPTER XV. —ARGUMENT FOR THE RESURRECTION FROM THE NATURE OF MAN.

But while the cause discoverable in the creation of men is of itself sufficient to prove that the resurrection follows by natural sequence on the dissolution of bodies, yet it is perhaps right not to shrink from adducing either of the proposed arguments, but, agreeably to what has been said, to point out to those who are not able of themselves to discern them, the arguments from each of the truths evolved from the primary; and first and foremost, the nature of the men created, which conducts us to the same notion, and has the same force as evidence of the resurrection. For if the whole nature of men in general is composed of an immortal soul and a body which was fitted to it in the creation, and if neither to the nature of the soul by itself, nor to the nature of the body separately, has God assigned such a creation or such a life and entire course of existence as this, but to men compounded of the two, in order that they may, when they have passed through their present existence, arrive at one common end, with the same elements of which they are composed at their birth and during life, it unavoidably follows, since one living-being is formed from the two, experiencing whatever the soul experiences and whatever the body experiences, doing and performing whatever requires the judgment of the senses or of the reason, that the whole series of these things must be referred to some one end, in order that they all, and by means of all,—namely, man's creation, man's nature, man's life, man's doings and sufferings, his course of existence, and the end suitable to his nature,— may concur in one harmony and the same common experience. But if there is some one harmony and community of experience belonging to the whole being, whether of the things which spring from the soul or of those which are accomplished by means of the body, the end for all these must also be one. And the end will be in strictness one, if the being whose end that end is remains the same in its constitution; and the being will be exactly the same, if all those things of which the being consists as parts are the same. And they will be the same in respect of their peculiar union, if the parts dissolved are again united for the constitution of the being. And the constitution of the same men of necessity proves that a resurrection will follow of the dead and dissolved bodies; for without this, neither could the same parts be united according to nature with one another, nor could the nature of the same men be reconstituted. And if both understanding and reason have been given to men for the discernment of things which are perceived by the understanding, and not of existences only, but also of the goodness and wisdom and rectitude of their Giver, it necessarily follows that, since those things continue for the sake of which the rational judgment is given, the judgment given for these things should also continue. But it is impossible for this to continue, unless the nature which has received it, and in which it adheres, continues. But that which has received both understanding and reason is man, not the soul by itself. Man, therefore, who consists of the two parts, must continue for ever. But it is impossible for him to continue unless he rise again. For if no resurrection were to take place, the nature of men as men would not continue. And if the nature of men does not continue, in vain has the soul been fitted to the need of the body and to its experiences; in vain has the body been fettered so that it cannot obtain what it longs for, obedient to the reins of the soul, and guided by it as with a bridle; in vain is the understanding, in vain is wisdom, and the observance of rectitude, or even the practice of every virtue, and the enactment and enforcement of laws,—to say all in a word, whatever is noble in men or for men's sake, or rather the very creation and nature of men. But if vanity is utterly excluded from all the works of God, and from all the gifts bestowed by Him, the conclusion is unavoidable, that, along with the interminable duration of the soul, there will be a perpetual continuance of the body according to its proper nature.

CHAPTER XVI—ANALOGY OF DEATH AND SLEEP, AND CONSEQUENT ARGUMENT FOR THE RESURRECTION.

And let no one think it strange that we call by the name of life a continuance of being which is interrupted by death and corruption; but let him consider rather that this word has not one meaning only, nor is there only one measure of continuance, because the nature also of the things that continue is not one. For if each of the things that continue has its continuance according to its peculiar nature, neither in the case of those who are wholly incorruptible and immortal shall we find the continuance like ours, because the natures of superior beings do not take the level of such as are inferior; nor in men is it proper to look for a continuance invariable and unchangeable; inasmuch as the former are from the first created immortal, and continue to exist without end by the simple will of their Maker, and men, in respect of the soul, have from their first origin an unchangeable continuance, but in respect of the body obtain immortality by means of change. This is what is meant by the doctrine of the resurrection; and, looking to this, we both await the dissolution of the body, as the sequel to a life of want and corruption, and after this we hope for a continuance with immortality, not putting either our death on a level with the death of the irrational animals, or the continuance of man with the continuance of immortals, lest we should unawares in this way put human nature and life on a level with things with which it is not proper to compare them. It ought not, therefore, to excite dissatisfaction, if some inequality appears to exist regarding the duration of men; nor, because the separation of the soul from the members of the body and the dissolution of its parts interrupts the continuity of life, must we therefore despair of the resurrection. For although the relaxation of the senses and of the physical powers, which naturally takes place in sleep, seems to interrupt the sensational life when men sleep at equal intervals of time, and, as it were, come back to life again, yet we do not refuse to call it life; and for this reason, I suppose, some call sleep the brother of death, not as deriving their origin from the same ancestors and fathers, but because those who are dead and those who sleep are subject to similar states, as regards at least the stillness and the absence of all sense of the present or the past, or rather of existence itself and their own life. If, therefore, we do not refuse to call by the name of life the life of men full of such inequality from birth to dissolution, and interrupted by all those things which we have before mentioned, neither ought we to despair of the life succeeding to dissolution, such as involves the resurrection, although for a time it is interrupted by the separation of the soul from the body.

CHAPTER XVII. —THE SERIES OF CHANGES WE CAN NOW TRACE IN MAN RENDERS A RESURRECTION PROBABLE.

For this nature of men, which has inequality allotted to it from the first, and according to the purpose of its Maker, has an unequal life and continuance, interrupted sometimes by sleep, at another time by death, and by the changes incident to each period of life, whilst those which follow the first are not clearly seen beforehand. Would any one have believed, unless taught by experience, that in the soft seed alike in all its parts there was deposited such a variety and number of great powers, or of masses, which in this way arise and become consolidated—I mean of bones, and nerves, and cartilages, of muscles too, and flesh, and intestines, and the other parts of the body? For neither in the yet moist seed is anything of this kind to be seen, nor even in infants do any of those things make their appearance which pertain to adults, or in the adult period what belongs to those who are past their prime, or in these what belongs to such as have grown old. But although some of the things I have said exhibit not at all, and others but faintly, the natural sequence and the changes that come upon the nature of men, yet all who are not blinded in their judgment of these matters by vice or sloth, know that there must be first the depositing of the seed, and that when this is completely organized in respect of every member and part and the progeny comes forth to the light, there comes the growth belonging to the first period of life, and the maturity which attends growth, and after the maturity the slackening of the physical powers till old age, and then, when the body is worn out, its dissolution. As, therefore, in this matter, though neither the seed has inscribed upon it the life or form of men, nor the life the dissolution into the primary elements; the succession of natural occurrences makes things credible which have no credibility from the phenomena themselves, much more does reason, tracing out the truth from the natural sequence, afford ground for believing in the resurrection, since it is safer and stronger than experience for establishing the truth.

CHAPTER XVIII. —JUDGMENT MUST HAVE REFERENCE BOTH TO SOUL AND BODY: THERE WILL THEREFORE BE A RESURRECTION.

The arguments I just now proposed for examination, as establishing the truth of the resurrection, are all of the same kind, since they all start from the same point; for their starting-point is the origin of the first men by creation. But while some of them derive their strength from the starting-point itself from which they take their rise, others, consequent upon the nature and the life of men, acquire their credibility from the superintendence of God over us; for the cause according to which, and on account of which, men have come into being, being closely connected with the nature of men, derives its force from creation; but the argument from rectitude, which represents God as judging men according as they have lived well or ill, derives its force from the end of their existence: they come into being on the former ground, but their state depends more on God's superintendence. And now that the matters which come first have been demonstrated by me to the best of my ability, it will be well to prove our proposition by those also which come after—I mean by the reward or punishment due to each man in accordance with righteous judgment, and by the final cause of human existence; and of these I put foremost that which takes the lead by nature, and inquire first into the argument relating to the judgment: premising only one thing, from concern for the principle which appertains to the matters before us, and for order—namely, that it is incumbent on those who admit God to be the Maker of this universe, to ascribe to His wisdom and rectitude the preservation and care of all that has been created, if they wish to keep to their own principles; and with such views to hold that nothing either in earth or in heaven is without guardianship or providence, but that, on the contrary, to everything, invisible and visible alike, small and great, the attention of the Creator reaches; for all created things require the attention of the Creator, and each one in particular, according to its nature and the end for which it was made: though I think it would be a useless expenditure of trouble to go through the list now, or distinguish between the several cases, or mention in detail what is suitable to each nature. Man, at all events, of whom it is now our business to speak, as being in want, requires food; as being mortal, posterity; as being rational, a process of judgment. But if each of these things belongs to man by nature, and he requires food for his life, and requires posterity for the continuance of the race, and requires a judgment in order that food and posterity may be according to law, it of course follows, since food and posterity refer to both together, that the judgment must be referred to them too (by both together I mean man, consisting of soul and body), and that such man becomes accountable for all his actions, and receives for them either reward or punishment. Now, if the righteous judgment awards to both together its retribution for the deeds wrought; and if it is not proper that either the soul alone should receive the wages of the deeds wrought in union with the body (for this of itself has no inclination to the faults which are committed in connection with the pleasure or food and culture of the body), or that the body alone should (for this of itself is incapable of distinguishing law and justice), but man, composed of these, is subjected to trial for each of the deeds wrought by him; and if reason does not find this happening either in this life (for the award according to merit finds no place in the present existence, since many atheists and persons who practice every iniquity and wickedness live on to the last, unvisited by calamity, whilst, on the contrary, those who have manifestly lived an exemplary life in respect of every virtue, live in pain, in insult, in calumny and outrage, and suffering of all kinds) or after death (for both together no longer exist, the soul being separated from the body, and the body itself being resolved again into the materials out of which it was composed, and no longer retaining anything of its former structure or form, much less the remembrance of its actions): the result of all this is very plain to every one,—namely, that, in the language of the apostle, "this corruptible (and dissoluble) must put on incorruption," in order that those who were dead, having been made alive by the resurrection, and the parts that were separated and entirely dissolved having been again united, each one may, in accordance with justice, receive what he has done by the body, whether it be good or bad.

CHAPTER XIX. —MAN WOULD BE MORE UNFAVOURABLY SITUATED THAN THE BEASTS IF THERE WERE NO RESURRECTION.

In replying, then, to those who acknowledge a divine superintendence, and admit the same principles as we do, yet somehow depart from their own admissions, one may use such arguments as those which have been adduced, and many more than these, should he be disposed to amplify what has been said only concisely and in a cursory manner. But in dealing with those who differ from us concerning primary truths, it will perhaps be well to lay down another principle antecedent to these, joining with them in doubting of the things to which their opinions relate, and examining the matter along with them in this manner—whether the life of men, and their entire course of existence, is overlooked, and a sort of dense darkness is poured down upon the earth, hiding in ignorance and silence both the men themselves and their actions; or whether it is much safer to be of opinion that the Maker presides over the things which He Himself has made, inspecting all things whatsoever which exist, or come into existence, Judge of both deeds and purposes. For if no judgment whatever were to be passed on the actions of men, men would have no advantage over the irrational creatures, but rather would fare worse than these do, inasmuch as they keep in subjection their passions, and concern themselves about piety, and righteousness, and the other virtues; and a life after the manner of brutes would be the best, virtue would be absurd, the threat of judgment a matter for broad laughter, indulgence in every kind of pleasure the highest good, and the common resolve of all these and their one law would be that maxim, so dear to the intemperate and lewd, "Let us eat and drink, for to-morrow we die." For the termination of such a life is not even pleasure, as some suppose, but utter insensibility. But if the Maker of men takes any concern about His own works, and the distinction is anywhere to be found between those who have lived well and ill, it must be either in the present life, while men are still living who have conducted themselves virtuously or viciously, or after death, when men are in a state of separation and dissolution. But according to neither of these suppositions can we find a just judgment taking place; for neither do the good in the present life obtain the rewards of virtue, nor yet do the bad receive the wages of vice. I pass over the fact, that so long as the nature we at present possess is preserved, the moral nature is not able to bear a punishment commensurate with the more numerous or more serious faults. For the robber, or ruler, or tyrant, who has unjustly put to death myriads on myriads, could not by one death make restitution for these deeds; and the man who holds no true opinion concerning God, but lives in all outrage and blasphemy, despises divine things, breaks the laws, commits outrage against boys and women alike, razes cities unjustly, burns houses with their inhabitants, and devastates a country, and at the same time destroys inhabitants of cities and peoples, and even an entire nation—how in a mortal body could he endure a penalty adequate to these crimes, since death prevents the deserved punishment, and the mortal nature does not suffice for any single one of his deeds? It is proved, therefore, that neither in the present life is there a judgment according to men's deserts, nor after death.

CHAPTER XX. —MAN MUST BE POSSESSED BOTH OF A BODY AND SOUL HEREAFTER, THAT THE JUDGMENT PASSED UPON HIM MAY BE JUST.

For either death is the entire extinction of life, the soul being dissolved and corrupted along with the body, or the soul remains by itself, incapable of dissolution, of dispersion, of corruption, whilst the body is corrupted and dissolved, retaining no longer any remembrance of past actions, nor sense of what it experienced in connection with the soul. If the life of men is to be utterly extinguished, it is manifest there will be no care for men who are not living, no judgment respecting those who have lived in virtue or in vice; but there will rush in again upon us whatever belongs to a lawless life, and the swarm of absurdities which follow from it, and that which is the summit of this lawlessness—atheism. But if the body were to be corrupted, and each of the dissolved particles to pass to its kindred element, yet the soul to remain by itself as immortal, neither on this supposition would any judgment on the soul take place, since there would be an absence of equity: for it is unlawful to suspect that any judgment can proceed out of God and from God which is wanting in equity. Yet equity *is* wanting to the judgment, if the being is not preserved in existence who practiced righteousness or lawlessness: for that which practiced each of the things in life on which the judgment is passed was man, not soul by itself. To sum up all in a word, this view will in no case consist with equity.

CHAPTER XXI. —CONTINUATION OF THE ARGUMENT.

For if good deeds are rewarded, the body will clearly be wronged, inasmuch as it has shared with the soul in the toils connected with well-doing, but does not share in the reward of the good deeds, and because, though the soul is often excused for certain faults on the ground of the body's neediness and want, the body itself is deprived of all share in the good deeds done, the toils on behalf of which it helped to bear during life. Nor, again, if faults are judged, is the soul dealt fairly with, supposing it alone to pay the penalty for the faults it committed through being solicited by the body and drawn away by it to its own appetites and motions, at one time being seized upon and carried off, at another attracted in some very violent manner, and sometimes concurring with it by way of kindness and attention to its preservation. How can it possibly be other than unjust for the soul to be judged by itself in respect of things towards which in its own nature it feels no appetite, no motion, no impulse, such as licentiousness, violence, covetousness, injustice, and the unjust acts arising out of these? For if the majority of such evils come from men's not having the mastery of the passions which solicit them, and they are solicited by the neediness and want of the body, and the care and attention required by it (for these are the motives for every acquisition of property, and especially for the using of it, and moreover for marriage and all the actions of life, in which things, and in connection with which, is seen what is faulty and what is not so), how can it be just for the soul alone to be judged in respect of those things which the body is the first to be sensible of, and in which it draws the soul away to sympathy and participation in actions with a view to things which it wants; and that the appetites and pleasures, and moreover the fears and sorrows, in which whatever exceeds the proper bounds is amenable to judgment, should be set in motion by the body, and yet that the sins arising from these, and the punishments for the sins committed, should fall upon the soul alone, which neither needs anything of this sort, nor desires nor fears or suffers of itself any such thing as man is wont to suffer? But even if we hold that these affections do not pertain to the body alone, but to man, in saying which we should speak correctly, because the life of man is one, though composed of the two, yet surely we shall not assert that these things belong to the soul, if we only look simply at its peculiar nature. For if it is absolutely without need of food, it can never desire those things which it does not in the least require for its subsistence; nor can it feel any impulse towards any of those things which it is not at all fitted to use; nor, again, can it be grieved at the want of money or other property, since these are not suited to it. And if, too, it is superior to corruption, it fears nothing whatever as destructive of itself: it has no dread of famine, or disease, or mutilation, or blemish, or fire, or sword, since it cannot suffer from any of these any hurt or pain, because neither bodies nor bodily powers touch it at all. But if it is absurd to attach the passions to the soul as belonging specially to it, it is in the highest degree unjust and unworthy of the judgment of God to lay upon the soul alone the sins which spring from them, and the consequent punishments.

CHAPTER XXII. —CONTINUATION OF THE ARGUMENT.

In addition to what has been said, is it not absurd that, while we cannot even have the notion of virtue and vice as existing separately in the soul (for we recognize the virtues as man's virtues, even as in like manner vice, their opposite, as not belonging to the soul in separation from the body, and existing by itself), yet that the reward or punishment for these should be assigned to the soul alone? How can any one have even the notion of courage or fortitude as existing in the soul alone, when it has no fear of death, or wounds, or maiming, or loss, or maltreatment, or of the pain connected with these, or the suffering resulting from them? And what shall we say of self-control and temperance, when there is no desire drawing it to food or sexual intercourse, or other pleasures and enjoyments, nor any other thing soliciting it from within or exciting it from without? And what of practical wisdom, when things are not proposed to it which may or may not be done, nor things to be chosen or avoided, or rather when there is in it no motion at all or natural impulse towards the doing of anything? And how in any sense can equity be an attribute of souls, either in reference to one another or to anything else, whether of the same or of a different kind, when they are not able from any source, or by any means, or in any way, to bestow that which is equal according to merit or according to analogy, with the exception of the honor rendered to God, and, moreover, have no impulse or motion towards the use of their own things, or abstinence from those of others, since the use of those things which are according to nature, or the abstinence from them, is considered in reference to those who are so constituted as to use them, whereas the soul neither wants anything, nor is so constituted as to use any things or any single thing, and therefore what is called the independent action of the parts cannot be found in the soul so constituted?

CHAPTER XXIII. —CONTINUATION OF THE ARGUMENT.

But the most irrational thing of all is this: to impose properly sanctioned laws on men, and then to assign to their souls alone the recompense of their lawful or unlawful deeds. For if he who receives the laws would also justly receive the recompense of the transgression of the laws, and if it was man that received the laws, and not the soul by itself, man must also bear the recompense for the sins committed, and not the soul by itself, since God has not enjoined on souls to abstain from things which have no relation to them, such as adultery, murder, theft, rapine, dishonor to parents, and every desire in general that tends to the injury and loss of our neighbors. For neither the command, "Honor thy father and thy mother," is adapted to souls alone, since such names are not applicable to them, for souls do not produce souls, so as to appropriate the appellation of father or mother, but men produce men; nor could the command, "Thou shalt not commit adultery," ever be properly addressed to souls, or even thought of in such a connection, since the difference of male and female does not exist in them, nor any aptitude for sexual intercourse, nor appetite for it; and where there is no appetite, there can be no intercourse; and where there is no intercourse at all, there can be no legitimate intercourse, namely marriage; and where there is no lawful intercourse, neither can there be unlawful desire of, or intercourse with, another man's wife, namely adultery. Nor, again, is the prohibition of theft, or of the desire of having more, applicable to souls, for they do not need those things, through the need of which, by reason of natural indigence or want, men are accustomed to steal or to rob, such as gold, or silver, or an animal, or something else adapted for food, or shelter, or use; for to an immortal nature everything which is desired by the needy as useful is useless. But let the fuller discussion of these matters be left to those who wish to investigate each point more exactly, or to contend more earnestly with opponents. But, since what has just been said, and that which concurs with this to guarantee the resurrection, suffices for us, it would not be seasonable to dwell any longer upon them; for we have not made it our aim to omit nothing that might be said, but to point out in a summary manner to those who have assembled what ought to be thought concerning the resurrection, and to adapt to the capacity of those present the arguments bearing on this question.

CHAPTER XXIV. —ARGUMENT FOR THE RESURRECTION FROM THE CHIEF END OF MAN.

The points proposed for consideration having been to some extent investigated, it remains to examine the argument from the end or final cause, which indeed has already emerged in what has been said, and only requires just so much attention and further discussion as may enable us to avoid the appearance of leaving unmentioned any of the matters briefly referred to by us, and thus indirectly damaging the subject or the division of topics made at the outset. For the sake of those present, therefore, and of others who may pay attention to this subject, it may be well just to signify that each of those things which are constituted by nature, and of those which are made by art, must have an end peculiar to itself, as indeed is taught us by the common sense of all men, and testified by the things that pass before our eyes. For do we not see that husbandmen have one end, and physicians another; and again, the things which spring out of the earth another, and the animals nourished upon it, and produced according to a certain natural series, another? If this is evident, and natural and artificial powers, and the actions arising from these, must by all means be accompanied by an end in accordance with nature, it is absolutely necessary that the end of men, since it is that of a peculiar nature, should be separated from community with the rest; for it is not lawful to suppose the same end for beings destitute of rational judgment, and of those whose actions are regulated by the innate law and reason, and who live an intelligent life and observe justice. Freedom from pain, therefore, cannot be the proper end for the latter, for this they would have in common with beings utterly devoid of sensibility: nor can it consist in the enjoyment of things which nourish or delight the body, or in an abundance of pleasures; else a life like that of the brutes must hold the first place, while that regulated by virtue is without a final cause. For such an end as this, I suppose, belongs to beasts and cattle, not to men possessed of an immortal soul and rational judgment.

CHAPTER XXV. —ARGUMENT CONTINUED AND CONCLUDED.

Nor again is it the happiness of soul separated from body: for we are not inquiring about the life or final cause of either of the parts of which man consists, but of the being who is composed of both; for such is every man who has a share in this present existence, and there must be some appropriate end proposed for this life. But if it is the end of both parts together, and this can be discovered neither while they are still living in the present state of existence through the numerous causes already mentioned, nor yet when the soul is in a state of separation, because the man cannot be said to exist when the body is dissolved, and indeed entirely scattered abroad, even though the soul continue by itself—it is absolutely necessary that the end of a man's being should appear in some reconstitution of the two together, and of the same living being. And as this follows of necessity, there must by all means be a resurrection of the bodies which are dead, or even entirely dissolved, and the same men must be formed anew, since the law of nature ordains the end not absolutely, nor as the end of any men whatsoever, but of the same men who passed through the previous life; but it is impossible for the same men to be reconstituted unless the same bodies are restored to the same souls. But that the same soul should obtain the same body is impossible in any other way, and possible only by the resurrection; for if this takes place, an end befitting the nature of men follows also. And we shall make no mistake in saying, that the final cause of an intelligent life and rational judgment, is to be occupied uninterruptedly with those objects to which the natural reason is chiefly and primarily adapted, and to delight unceasingly in the contemplation of *Him who is*, and of His decrees, notwithstanding that the majority of men, because they are affected too passionately and too violently by things below, pass through life without attaining this object. For the large number of those who fail of the end that belongs to them does not make void the common lot, since the examination relates to individuals, and the reward or punishment of lives ill or well spent is proportioned to the merit of each.

www.ingramcontent.com/pod-product-compliance
Lightning Source LLC
Chambersburg PA
CBHW052110070526
44584CB00017B/2415